Biblical Balance
on
Submission and Authority

Biblical Balance
on
Submission and Authority

A. JOHN CARR

Foreword by Cecil Cousen

CHARIS PUBLICATIONS
58 CONSTITUTION STREET
DUNDEE, SCOTLAND
DD3 6NE
Telephone (0382) 26372

Printed in Scotland U.K. for Charis Publications
by Geo. E. Findlay & Co. Ltd., Dundee.

To
My Father and Mother
who have set a shining example
of faithfulness and devotion for
all their grateful family to follow.

All scripture quotations are from
the Authorised Version unless
otherwise stated.

Cover illustration by Stan Clementsmith

Contents

Acknowledgments

I am most grateful to Cecil Cousen for writing the Foreword and for his encouragement through the years. Also to Pastor James McLure who was used by the Lord to introduce me to our fellowship in Dundee in 1963 where many of the principles expounded in this book have been patiently learned in practical ways. Special thanks go to Miss Florence Mulvie who has typed the script at least three times, and my cousin Philip and son Stuart who diligently applied themselves to editing and correcting the text.

Foreword

I have known John for many years. Though still in the prime of life he is already a distinguished looking Welsh divine!—as Proverbs has it *A hoary head is a crown of glory; it is gained in a righteous life.* This is true of John. Perhaps some at least of his white hairs are the result of his exposure to conflict and controversy in the realm of authority. Nevertheless his experiences have not left him with a chip on his shoulder, but have rather produced a 'Welsh divine' indeed, with an outflowing ministry of which this book is a fine example; all of which underlines that the book is not theoretical, though intensely Biblical, but thoroughly practical, born from personal experience and long Bible study.

This book is written in the context of the spirit of the age which in many areas has invaded the professing Church, the spirit of lawlessness, rebellion and couldn't-care-less-ness. It is also written in the context of 'Renewal'. Most previous Renewals have ultimately produced new divisions in the Body of Christ; this book—and the whole emphasis of 'the charismatic movement' for its first 15 years—is a strong plea that this time Renewal will produce a coming-together in oneness in the Body of Christ. Indeed, the book is as much about 'the Body of Christ' as about its titled subject. And very good teaching too.

Although in no way judgemental, nor advocating any rush to re-structure, it is nevertheless made clear that many of the reasons for our fragmented Church stem from imbalance in the areas of authority and submission.

A few central themes keep cropping up in different contexts. Perhaps this repetition has something to do with the author's Welsh love of 'wordiness', or is it that these few fundamental issues need to be said again and again to get the point home—an example of the modern phrase: 'You can say that again'. For instance, if a leader and flock alike will submit themselves 'one to the other in the fear of the Lord' then true fellowship in the Body will be fostered and enjoyed in the Holy Spirit. Or again, there is a constant and healthy insistence that any and every authority in the Church belong only to the risen Christ who is Head of the Body; and can only be expressed through His people in the same spirit of humility, love and caring evident in the Master's ministry and which equally manifest the Master's victory over the power of sin and darkness.

To illustrate let me quote: *In the Psalms we have a beautiful prophetic insight into the day of God's power when Christ's Church is seen to be standing together as an army in holy array, expressing the authority of the risen, ascended Lord and manifesting a royal priestly ministry in the Name of Him who has an eternally unchanging priesthood. Both the Lordship and priesthood of Christ are reflected in God's willing people. They are seen as His united Church joined to Christ its Head. Through the Church He rules and reigns in the midst of His enemies. What a picture of His totally victorious, overcoming Church.*

CECIL COUSEN

P.S. I have not mentioned the central theme: the two extremes of imbalance. You will enjoy finding out what these are—maybe in an uncomfortable kind of way!

Preface

Where there is no vision the people perish. But the Church is **not** without vision and it shall **not** fail. Those who are in tune with the Holy Spirit are receiving insight into God's unfolding purpose for these momentous times. The measure of revelation which I have received has produced within me a yearning to share its message, so that faith will spring up in the hearts of all God's people to believe for, and to experience its fulfilment. I feel grieved in spirit when I observe the many unnecessary obstacles hindering its realisation.

This has prompted me to take up my pen once again to examine some of these problems in the light of God's Word. I have no desire to be vindictive in exposing any imbalances in current thinking and practice in the area of submission and authority, but I have a deep longing to see the Church united under the Headship of Christ. Even with the sincerest of motives, most of us have blundered somewhere along the line in endeavouring to fulfil our calling. But the Lord is patient and longsuffering and readily responds to repentance and submissiveness by putting us back on course.

If we discover that we have erred, let us be humble enough to admit it, and in turning from our error, experience God's forgiveness and find ourselves once again in the flow of His glorious purpose.

The apostle Paul exhorts us to give no place to the devil. As long as the Church remains divided and fragmented, we are providing ground for exploitation by the enemy. Once we recognise our need of fellowship and are willing to learn from each other we will be less susceptible to Satan's strategy.

12

The unity of the Church will come, for Jesus has said: *I will build my church, and the gates of hell shall not prevail against it.* My sincere prayer is that this book will be read in the spirit in which it has been written and that fellow-believers everywhere will experience the liberty and enrichment which God intends for us all.

I have not pursued an exhaustive study of all the questions that the subject of this book may raise. To have done that would undoubtedly have obscured the basic principles which I have sought to underline.

It may be felt that some statements and Scripture quotations have been repeated more often than would seem appropriate, and that unnecessary references are made to issues early in the book which are given fuller treatment in later chapters. This approach has been used so that truths will be understood within the context of each individual chapter.

Thanks be to God our Father and to our Lord Jesus Christ who is Head over **all things** to the Church, which is His Body.

A. JOHN CARR.

Dundee,
Scotland.

21st October, 1982.

1

Restoration

These are momentous days. On one hand we are witnessing the disintegration of human society and the dissolution of its institutions and systems. On the other we give thanks to God that by the outpouring of His Holy Spirit the miracle of the emerging Church is taking place.

This is a most exciting era for the whole Body of Christ. We are privileged to witness and experience worldwide the fulfilment of the prophecy of Joel—*In the last days . . . I will pour out of my spirit upon all flesh.*[1] Everywhere, in every nation, renewed, Spirit-filled believers are singing:

All over the world the Spirit is moving,

All over the world as the prophet said it would be,

All over the world there's a mighty revelation,

Of the glory of the Lord as the waters cover the sea.

Regardless of denomination or background, believers are experiencing the manifestation of spiritual gifts. Various ministries and functions are being restored. Church leaders are receiving revelation concerning the specific gifts that the ascended Christ gave to the Church—of apostles, prophets, evangelists, pastors and teachers. Whilst our systems are crumbling, these ministries are developing so that the saints will be perfected and matured to fulfil the function for which each one is called. In this way the whole Body will be built up *till we all come in the unity of the faith, and of the knowledge of the Son of God, unto a perfect man, unto the measure of the stature*

[1] Acts 2:17.

of the fulness of Christ.[1]

It is inevitable, therefore, that radical and major changes should affect the Christian Church. Historically, especially since the dawn of the reformation, every fresh move of the Spirit of God has produced a revival of New Testament principles of faith and practice. Now much stress is being laid on the importance of discipleship, shepherding, submission and authority, and new concepts concerning these neglected truths are being propagated amongst the people of God everywhere. Sadly, these are often misunderstood and misapplied with the result that, for some, there is further disillusionment, and for the Church, continuing fragmentation and division.

[1] Eph. 4:13.

2

Signs of Imbalance

What are these problems? What light does the Word of God throw on them? In this book I have addressed myself to these matters. Here are some of the more disturbing ones.

Authoritarianism

The danger exists of hierarchical authority lording over the flock and seeking to assert dominion over their faith. Some who are called leaders, shepherds or apostles, all of which are valid scriptural nominations can, in the flesh, dominate, dictate, control and subjugate the members. If, even in the slightest degree, the pre-eminence of Christ in His Lordship and Headship is usurped, then such behaviour is unscriptural and dangerous.

Subjugation

Such authoritarianism leads to subjugation of the individual's will and personality. He may be deprived of the right to make personal and domestic decisions without prior consultation with his appointed authority. He will be expected, and in some cases, demanded to give unquestioning, robot-like submission to his leader. He may be discouraged from knowing and hearing God for himself, because his shepherd hears God for him. Any independent decision made or action taken by the individual, even in personal and domestic matters, without submitting it first to his leader is treated as rebellion. The individual is instructed that, even if the leader is wrong, he is to submit and that the responsibility and accountability is the leader's and not his personal concern.

Fear

The in-word is 'Commitment', for true fellowship means that we commit ourselves to God and to one another. When, however, commitment means that we make a life-time covenant to a leader, or group, or one another, serious problems can arise. If, for instance, such covenant vows are demanded of believers when they are young in the faith and spiritually immature, and in their subsequent more enlightened and mature state they see the error of such vows and wish to be free, what are the consequences of any action they may take to accomplish this? In some cases, the history of the subjugation of the individual's mind and will, the treatment of rejection, excommunication and judgemental pronouncements by former leaders produce such terrible fears that it has taken some people a long time and much compassionate and anointed ministry to liberate them from the bondage.

Exclusivism

Commitment in fellowship is scriptural and right, for experience shows how lack of commitment leads to non-co-ordination, distrust, indiscipline and carelessness. Sometimes, however, demands are made for a degree of commitment to leaders or groups that inhibits and discourages open fellowship with other believers. Such organisations tend to become so exclusive that they only recognise anointed ministries within the committed grouping, and their actions and attitudes reveal that they refuse to respect or accept anointed ministries not committed directly to them.

All the above seems exceedingly negative. But there are some good and positive things relating to responsible leadership such as: the true discipline of discipleship, the nature and necessity of spiritual authority and the scriptural meaning of submission to one another in the Body of Christ. When we come to look at these I pray that the extreme, carnal structures arising today will be seen for what they are so that all will rejoice to see the Church of Christ emerge—beautiful and glorious—just as our Lord intends it to be.

This is not a time to fear, but to seek the face of God more fully so that we will be more discerning and better able to understand what the will of the Lord is. While there is conflict in some areas, let us not be alarmed. God is alerting His Church to new, important aspects of what fellowship and right relationships in the Body of Christ are about. Now is the time to give specific heed to the prayer of Jesus and believe for faith to spring up in all our hearts for the fulfilment of that prayer— *That they all may be one, as thou Father art in me, and I in thee, that they may be one in us, that the world may believe that thou hast sent me.*[1]

We cannot deny that there has been a lot of confusion, schism and fragmentation afflicting Christian people everywhere. This has left the Church weakened in its testimony, ineffective in its authority, and almost powerless to bring conviction to a Godless world. But faith is now springing up in the hearts of God's people. Vision is being restored. A new understanding of the Headship of Christ is capturing the hearts and minds of the people of God. They are seeing afresh that He is truly *Head over all things to the Church, which is his body, the fulness of him who filleth all in all.*[2] Good must come out of all the chaos because Jesus said *I will build my church, and the gates of hell shall not prevail against it.*[3]

With this restoration by the Holy Spirit, members of the Body of Christ within particular groups are flowing together in fellowship as never before. Better still, there are very clear signs that at long last members of different groups are experiencing an

[1] John 17:21. [2] Eph. 1:23. [3] Matt. 16:18.

impartation of divine grace that enables them to fellowship together, freed from the traditional barriers that previously hindered them.

When we receive a revelation of the glory of the grace of God which should manifestly characterise every member of the Body of Christ, we will begin to appreciate the uniqueness of what God has wrought in Christ for all his people. We will then cease pulling down God's Church and demeaning and denigrating the glory of the grace of God in the believers. We shall have a new appreciation of one another. Criticism and censure will end and, in the grace of the Lord Jesus, we shall praise God for one another; we shall edify, strengthen and encourage one another by our mutual faith.

The Church will be seen for what God has called it to be: purchased with great price, in *that Christ so loved the church that he gave himself for it.*[1] We shall recognise that we are not our own for we are bought with a price, the precious blood of Christ.[2] By the spirit of wisdom and revelation we will have our eyes opened to behold the riches of the glory of God's inheritance in the saints.[3] We will cease from grovelling as worms of the dust, and arise, not in human pride, but as the sons of God, to be the revelation of the glory of God's grace.[4] It is this grace that makes us, as God's people, accepted in the Beloved. In other words, as Mary was declared to be *highly favoured*[5] of the Lord, so is His Church in being the vehicle for bringing forth Christ in His fulness for all the world to behold.

All members of the Body of Christ know God the Father through Jesus Christ their Saviour and Lord, for *truly our fellowship is with the Father and with his Son Jesus Christ.*[6] On this basis, if we walk in the light as He is in the light, we have fellowship one with another, and His blood goes on making us clean. It is in this sense of open fellowship that we understand the exhortation of the apostle Paul in Ephesians 5:21 *Submitting yourselves one to another in the fear of God.*

[1] Eph. 5:25. [2] 1 Cor. 6:19, 20. [3] Eph. 1:17, 18. [4] Eph. 1:6. [5] Luke 1:28. [6] 1 John 1:3.

Tragically, for centuries much of what has called itself 'the Church' has been terribly fragmented because mostly its members related to each other *in the flesh*. All the works of the flesh enmity, strife, jealousy, anger, selfishness, covetousness, divisiveness, factions with party spirit, etc. have been characteristic of much of the Church's life and behaviour.[1] The question and indictment brought by the apostle Paul to the Galatian Church has been very prophetic of the unfolding history of the Church: *Having begun in the Spirit, are ye now made perfect by the flesh?*[2] Now that the Spirit of God is being poured out and people are beginning to walk and relate, no longer in the flesh but in the Spirit, we should expect to see all the precious fruit of the Spirit of God manifest amongst the fellowships of believers.

[1] Gal. 5:19, 20. [2] Gal. 3:3.

3

Fellowship in the Spirit

For a long time many sincere believers have almost despaired as they beheld their fellow-Christians engrossed in these works and attitudes of the flesh. Some have even questioned the vision of a mature, united Church expressing the fulness of Christ in His Body, and wondered if it were merely an idealistic concept both impractical and impossible in this life; a beautiful prospect to be realised perhaps in the glory-land. This mode of thinking tends to lead to the conclusion that the Church can experience only decline and demise and that the near return of the Lord is the only ray of hope on the horizon. How demoralising this is to many precious believers who are deprived of any vision for the Church on earth.

We can praise the Lord that we do not have to wait until then. The vision is for here and now. We are seeing afresh that fellowship is being restored, not on the basis of carnal, divisive attitudes which are but the works of the flesh, but of life in the Holy Spirit. We are beginning to understand the meaning of submitting one to another in the fear of God.

This can only begin with us as individuals. Each one of us must ask himself the question 'Is my fellowship, my relationship, my contribution in the Church promoting true fellowship amongst the members of the Body of Christ, or is it dividing, fragmenting and discouraging proper fellowship that is of the Spirit?' The rightness of relationships in the corporate fellowship of the Body of Christ depends essentially upon the right relationship of each of us with the Lord. The life stream from that then flows out towards all our brothers and sisters. Submission to God is essentially a personal and individual matter. Once that is in order there will be no problem in relationships with one another in the Body.

This relationship of one to another as members in the Body of Christ is unity of a special kind. When Jesus prayed *That they all may be one,*[1] He was praying for that essential unity that exists between Father and Son: *As thou, Father, art in me, and I in thee.* This unity is inextricably bound up in the life of the Father and Son. This is what the Holy Spirit is doing in the Church, for by Him we share in the very life of the Godhead: *That they may be one* **in us.** That is the teaching of the apostle Paul: *For by one Spirit are we all baptised into one body, whether we be Jew or Gentile, whether we be bond or free, and have been all made to drink into one Spirit.*[2] Therefore the unity of the Spirit is impossible unless our fellowship is with the Father and with His Son Jesus Christ the Lord. No councils or organisations of man can bring this about.

This should cause a cry to come from all our hearts: "Lord, show us how we can, by the Spirit, relate together aright, and **flow together** in the unity of the Spirit. Show us what it means to let the blessing of that **flow over** the divisions that separate us from one another, and **flow out** to bless our brothers and sisters, both in our locality and beyond." We can also thank God that there are very real signs of this happening, and be assured that God's Church will yet emerge to be the revelation of Christ in all His glorious fulness according to His eternal purpose.

This unity of the Spirit, which is sharing imparted divine life together, does not necessarily have to be organised, nor do we have to struggle with it. It does not become burdensome. If we are just trying to put things together and get together merely out of a sense of duty, we are struggling to fulfil in the flesh what was intended to be wrought in and among us by the Holy Spirit.

[1] John 17:21. [2] 1 Cor. 12:13.

In no way does this mean that we have to be careless and in-different about the unity of the Spirit. In fact, there is a clear apostolic appeal to us all to walk as becomes those who are called with a holy calling. We are to be aware of our responsibility one to another, and of the effect we have on each other.[1]

So we must apply ourselves diligently to keeping the unity of the Spirit in the bond of peace. This does not imply a struggle, nor should it create tension. Such endeavour should be a delight and not just an obligation. It will be a spontaneous flow because the Spirit of God has created the basic life and essence of the unity within us. Everything within us will yearn for its fulfilment among all the members of the Body of Christ. This is not a case of 'let us get together, for unity is strength.' That is the organised unity of the club or political party. The unity of the Spirit brings forth the beauty and the glory of Christ in all His wonderful fulness.

In the beginnings of the early Church the members were truly moving in the life of the Spirit. They did not only seek blessing, power and inspiration for themselves alone. The whole Body was blessed, and it moved in God with kingdom life, authority and power mightily in evidence. The whole Church corporately enjoyed the blessing of the life of the Spirit and members found that by love they could serve one another. Fellow-believers were encouraged, strengthened, edified and blessed. They were taught that the fruit of the Spirit: love, joy, peace, longsuffering, gentleness, goodness, meekness, faith, and self-control was theirs, not just for their own personal standing before God, but to enable them to relate together in proper fellowship. They were thus empowered by the Spirit to have right attitudes, motives and conduct toward one another.

Submitting yourselves one to another in the fear of God[2] is not a legalistic requirement. The context shows that this is the outflow from the ongoing Spirit-filled life. We can do this only

[1] Eph. 4: 1-7. [2] Eph. 5:21.

by the power of the Holy Spirit. When we are submitted to God there is no problem submitting to one another out of love for Christ with godly reverence and fear. This way fellowship is a joy. Troubles will still assail us but we will share them together. The enemy of our souls will seek to afflict and oppress us, but we will be covered by the power of the Spirit flowing through one another; as we stand by each other; as we pray for one another; as we seek to lift one another up in faith, in prayer and in the power of the Holy Ghost. The enemy will rage but we will be able to stand against him together and see him routed.

Those who fail to see that such unity can come to the Church here on earth, and who thus declare that this will be fulfilled only when we arrive in glory with our Lord, are in one sense right. Part of the Body of Christ is already there anyway and, until we are united with them, full and perfect unity cannot be realised. But why did Jesus pray *That they all may be one, as Thou, Father, art in me, and I in thee?*[1] Jesus Himself supplies the answer: *That the world might believe that thou hast sent me.* This just has to relate to the Church here on earth.

[1] John 17:21.

4

Biblical Submission and Authority

This question of submission and authority in the Church is amply dealt with by the apostle Peter. He instructs those who are elders to tend and feed the flock of God; to take the oversight thereof willingly, lovingly, and not at any time to be as lords over God's heritage, but rather to lead by example.[1] In the spirit of that he exhorts, *Ye younger, submit yourselves unto the elder.*[2] Why does the apostle Peter give this exhortation? It is because those who are older in the faith and who have been entrusted with responsibility for tending and feeding the flock of God are expected to give instruction, guidance and covering to those who are young in the faith.

But he also exhorts, *Yea, all of you be subject one to another, and be clothed with humility: for God resisteth the proud, and giveth grace to the humble.*[3] That call is not to the young and immature but to all. This includes those who have shepherding care over the members of the Body no matter who they are or what their function or responsibility is in the Body. If there is a spirit of pride in an individual and he cannot submit to others in the Body, God's blessing will not be upon his life. It is impossible for him to continue in the anointing of the Holy Spirit for God does not encourage and bless the proud but rather resists them. Make no mistake, this is one of the greatest dangers among leaders in the Church. The spirit of pride is utterly foreign to the life that is in Christ.

To the humble, however, grace is given. All that is required to

[1] 1 Peter 5:2-4. [2] 1 Peter 5:5. [3] 1 Peter 5:5.

make us the people that God has called us to be is included in His grace. Whatever our calling or stewardship; whatever our problems in relationships; God gives grace to the humble.

Submission to the immature

We should not fear that this principle of submission will result in us becoming unbalanced. God is not going to demand those who are mature to submit unquestioningly to instruction and direction by those who are less mature. Those who have been given stewardship and responsibility for overseeing the flock of God carry a spiritual authority. Such spiritual authority is easily recognised as it will always bear all the marks of the life of the Spirit with humility and grace. These are things we will be looking at later in the book.

This teaching from the Word of *submitting yourselves one to another in the fear of God,* and *being subject one to another* has caused problems for some. In the Church we have become so used to doing as we desire, that sometimes individuals have separated themselves from others to pursue a very independent course of action. Others have embarked on ventures merely to promote their own concept of Church life, ecclesiasticism or denominationalism. The resulting organisation often turns out to be exclusive and divisive, and not in the general flow of what the Spirit of God is doing.

Do we submit only to God?

We may assume that we are already in submission to God. We may even consider it to be very spiritual to say "I do not submit to man, I am interested only in submitting my life to God." There were actually people like that in Corinth. Some said *I am of Paul,* others said *I am of Apollos,* and others said *I am of Christ.*[1] But it is just as carnal to say that we are submitted to Christ and insubmissive to others as vice versa.

[1] 1 Cor. 1:12.

Be filled with the Spirit

Once we experience true submission to God and are filled with the Spirit, we have the life of God within us and walk in the Spirit. We walk in the grace, power and strength of the Spirit of God. Only then can we understand the true significance of submitting ourselves one to another in the fear of God. Submission to one another in the fear of God is directly related to 'going on being filled' [1] with the Holy Spirit. Therefore, if we are to enjoy the continuous infilling of the Spirit, it is imperative that we be submissive in the fellowship of the Body of Christ. If we are dedicated to God, He will honour, bless and anoint us with His Holy Spirit. It is those of us who are continually being filled with the Spirit who are enjoined to be submitting ourselves to one another in the fear of God.

The characteristics of this kind of submission should be manifest in believers, whatever their setting or function in the Body of Christ. To ignore this is to open the door to arrogance and pride. The Word of God outlines the evidences to be found in all who willingly, and in grace, submit one to another in the fear of God. Unity, openness, respect, trust, care, love, service, discipline, edification are some of these. Let us look at them in more detail.

---

[1] Eph. 5:18 (literal translation).

5

Unity

For by one Spirit are we all baptised into one body, whether we be Jew or Gentile, whether we be bond or free; and have been all made to drink into one Spirit.[1]

If we are filled with or baptised in the Holy Spirit then we live our life in God; in His purpose; in His power; in His love; in His blessing and in all that He is. To be baptised in the Spirit means that we are living our life in the power of the Spirit and we become increasingly aware that the Holy Spirit has come to immerse us all into one Body.

Relationships

How can we possibly live our individual personal lives in the Spirit and not properly relate together? It is not really conceivable, because one of the vital things the Holy Spirit has come to fulfil is to make the Body one. By one Spirit are we all baptised into one Body. If we are in the Spirit we will know how utterly important it is to understand that. When in conversation, dialogue or gossip, things are said that militate against that unity, the Holy Spirit is grieved and those who are walking in the Spirit will be grieved also, for *he that is joined unto the Lord is one spirit.*[2]

Those who are truly filled with the Spirit will never be content to see disunity in the Body, and will want no part in the furtherance of gossip and slander that promotes it. To such people, the divisions and disruptions that afflict the Church of

[1] 1 Cor. 12:13. [2] 1 Cor. 6:17.

Jesus Christ are a constant source of dismay.

Submission means unity

The apostle Paul beseeches every member of the Body of Christ to endeavour earnestly to keep the unity of the Spirit in the bond of peace.[1] This is the unity that only the Holy Spirit can create. This unity is spoken of here in terms of *one body*. This is what submitting one to another in the fear of God is concerned with. It is about being clothed with humility and being subject one to another. It is not just a legalistic demand, but rather the outflow of that which comes from the inflow of the Spirit. The Spirit of God within us will produce the gracious fruit of love, joy, peace and so on. Those with such fruit-bearing lives are not content to occupy a pew in a Church building but will know their setting in the Body and how they are fitly joined to the rest of the members. They will function in co-ordination with others.

When we are moving in the fulness of the Holy Spirit everything about our living, our relating, our attitudes and our conduct will be geared to the promoting of unity in the Body of Christ. The life of the Spirit in us desires this unity and urges us on to its fulfilment. There comes within us a constraint of love to see the Body being one.

Coping with each other

To submit one to another means that we are willing to *forbear with one another in love* for the purpose of keeping the unity. This is not possible in the flesh, for the flesh desires to assert and justify itself. The flesh will maintain 'my way is right, and what I declare is justifiable. I am going to have my way and nobody is going to tell me what to do.' That is why we must have the Spirit of God impart to us the very nature and grace of our Lord Jesus.

[1] Eph. 4:1-3.

Co-ordination of members

A body functions properly only when all its limbs and organs are co-ordinating together and are united to the head. Similarly, it is this principle alone which promotes effective and fruitful service in the lives of Christian believers. The Word of God teaches that the Church is the Body of Christ. This is one of the finest analogies of what the Church really is: a body with all its members properly joined together and the whole united with Christ, the Head. Thus, all the members are seen to be growing up together into Christ, in whom each one functions co-ordinatedly with the express purpose of building up the Body so that spontaneous life-flowing increase develops from itself.

The unity of the body, then, is every limb and organ in its rightful setting. Each one, whether complex or simple, is different and unique, yet vital to the whole. In this way the various parts of the body can be described as submitting to each other: fingers to the hand; the hand to the arm; the arm to the shoulder; the shoulder to the neck, and all joined to the head. If there is not this unity it is not a body, but a collection of limbs and organs.

Submission means fellowship

Do not be afraid of that good Bible word 'submission': it is the proper, humble way in which people are joined together in fellowship. It is, in fact, another descriptive word for fellowship and is an expression of the humility that God has wrought in us. By it we acknowledge our abandonment of life in the old nature, i.e. in the flesh with all its self-centred, independent and exclusive attitudes. We are new creations and we belong together as the family of God and the Body of Christ.

If we contemplate going off on our own to do something for God in the belief that we can achieve better results independently of fellowship, then no matter how right it may appear, it is not the purpose of God. Each individual member needs the others, and in submitting to one another we acknowledge our oneness together, our need of each other, and our own particular setting in the Body.

The prayer of Jesus

It is my firm conviction that the prayer of Jesus will be answered and that many of us will be privileged to witness its fulfilment. Until then the world will just continue to pass by and treat the Church with scorn. When the Church comes together in the unity of the Spirit it will then be able to face the community. The world will be reproved by the Spirit of God [1] through the members and become increasingly aware that Jesus Christ is real and was sent to this world by God the Father.[2] While the Church does not bring forth that kind of revelation to the community it is doing its own thing and is not subject to Christ its Head, nor are its members to one another.

All the potential for the fulfilment of that prayer of Jesus is already in His Church. For far too long we have believed the devil's lies and deceptions that we will never make it; that we are inadequate; that it is not possible to see the fulfilment of that prayer while we are here on earth. Now, by the Spirit of God, we are being enlightened; the enemy's strategy is being exposed; we are refusing to accept his lies and are beginning to believe God for the fulfilment of all that He has purposed among His people.

Uniqueness of each member

Unity in the Body does not mean that all members do the same thing, or the different parts of the Body operate in the same way. Each member is distinctive and unique, and has his own special setting and function. No part of the Body can perform as efficiently and thoroughly as the part intended and designed for that particular operation. Find your setting and know where you belong in the Body. Submit there, and begin to function in and

[1] John 16:8. [2] John 17:21.

by the grace that God has given you, for *He has given to every one grace according to the measure of the gift of Christ.*[1]

In the epistle to the Romans Paul gives a clear picture of the oneness of the Body; of the uniqueness and distinctiveness of each individual member in that Body; and yet the importance of the interdependence of each one.[2] We see that this does not rob us of our individuality. We are enabled by God's grace to fulfil our distinctive calling, but it can only be fully wrought in mutual dependence. Every ministry in the Body complements other ministries. If we recognise this principle and give ourselves to this unity, then we shall see the Body of Christ functioning as it is designed to do.

Our heart's cry

Do you yearn to see the Body of Christ functioning in this way? Do you long to witness the operation of all the gifts of the Spirit: word of wisdom, word of knowledge, faith, healings, miracles, discerning of spirits, tongues, interpretation, prophecy?[3] Does your heart cry to behold, not only manifestations of the Spirit, but the members themselves recognised as being gifts of the ascended Christ to the Body?

Specific gifts of apostles, prophets, evangelists, pastors, teachers, elders and deacons will provide anointed leadership so that all members will be released to function in their rightful calling and setting. The traditional concept that all ministry is the responsibility of the leadership is contrary to scriptural teaching. God intends that every member should minister to the Body. Apostles, prophets, evangelists, pastors and teachers are given to the Church so that the saints will be equipped to fulfil their work of service so that the whole Body will be edified or built up, *till we all come in the unity of the faith . . . unto the measure of the stature of the fulness of Christ.*[4]

[1] Eph. 4:7. [2] Romans 12. [3] 1 Cor. 12:7-11. [4] Eph. 4:11-13.

6

Openness

Now the Lord is that Spirit; and where the Spirit of the Lord is, there is liberty. But we all, with open face beholding as in a glass the glory of the Lord, are changed into the same image (into the same likeness) from glory to glory, even as by the Spirit of the Lord . . .[1]

One of the most lovely terms in the New Testament is *open face*. Paul in his defence before king Agrippa said *This thing was not done in a corner.*[2] In our fellowship with God and one another we should have nothing to hide. To submit one to another in the fear of God means to *walk in the light as He is in the light.*[3] Then, *we have fellowship one with another.*

Should we try to preserve our self-image?

An *open face* is the result of fellowship that springs from walking in the light of God. With nothing to hide we can look straight into the eyes of our brother and sister and behold purity, openness and honesty of heart, for in such fellowship there is nothing ulterior, dubious, or underhand. Here we see an unveiled, unmasked face. Often we are guilty of seeking to create a false impression that we are something other than our true selves. We seek to preserve our self-image, or the image that others have formed of us. This is not being open-faced. We are hiding behind a mask.

[1] 2 Cor. 3:17-4:2. [2] Acts 26:26. [3] 1 John 1:7.

How should we regard other fellowships in our area?

Some have gone into areas and situations where there is already a Christian testimony. Because it does not carry the label of their denomination, or promote those things to which they subscribe, they move in by stealth or without due openness and honesty. The Christian testimony is thus brought into disregard because suspicion and resentment arise between leaders and members of the Body of Christ. Divisions and animosities emerge and the unity of the Spirit is marred. This is the opposite of submitting to one another. *God is light, and in Him is no darkness at all,*[1] so true fellowship with Him will cause us to walk in light and truth with each other. Once we are known for this, people will trust us.

Lack of openness and honesty in all relationships in the Body of Christ creates barriers in people's minds and causes fragmentation of fellowship. We are not walking in the light of God if this situation exists. Walking in the light of God means that we behold and reflect the glory of our Lord Jesus, and are being changed into the same likeness.

I recall an incident when an imposter evangelist had deceived me through my spiritual naivety and lack of discernment. I learned of the deception through consultation with another pastor. Distressed by the discovery, I wondered if I could ever trust anyone again. At a prayer meeting my spirit was so low that I felt unable to pray. Finally I got to prayer and received a fresh vision of Jesus. My whole thinking was transported from the deception and corruption of this imposter to the trustworthiness, truth and honesty of my Lord and Master. For the very first time I understood the chorus 'His great beauty has completely won my heart', for I never had been able to associate beauty with the Manhood of Christ. Now I realised it was the beauty and glory of His innate character that was so perfect, pure and good. This brought a new relationship of love between

[1] 1 John 1:5.

my Lord and me that I had never known in such depth before. Now I could see the contrast between the subtle strategy of satanic deception and the open trustworthiness, loveliness and transparency of my Lord. It lifted me out of my distress.

In my experiences of dealing with many and varied demonic activities in people's lives, I have consistently discovered a very real cover up operation. A person who has submitted to devilish practices, when confronted by the authority of the Lordship of Christ in the believer, will not be able to look him straight in the face. The eyes are shifty and unsteady. All satan's work is characterised by deception, and is wrought in darkness. We are commanded to *have no fellowship with the unfruitful works of darkness.*[1] Is it not unthinkable, then, that God's people should identify with any underhand activity in their relationships and practice? To submit one to another in the fear of God must involve being open-faced before each other.

In this light, says the apostle Paul, *we have renounced the hidden things of dishonesty, not walking in craftiness, nor handling the word of God deceitfully; but by manifestation of the truth commending ourselves to every man's conscience in the sight of God.*[2]

Satan's kingdom cannot stand the openness of face wrought in the believer by the liberating work of the Spirit of God. It is foreign to his whole nature. He is a deceiver and a liar, and all his works are characterised by deception. We have been translated from the power of darkness into the kingdom of God's dear Son. He *is light, and in Him is no darkness at all.* Those who are thus transformed by the Spirit of God will not want to walk in darkness nor hide from others, but will desire to be open, loving, kind, patient and longsuffering.

Our conduct as members of the Body of Christ is all important. Whatever our ministry, there should be nothing to hide. Paul said that they, the apostles, had not merely given up

[1] Eph. 5:11. [2] 2 Cor. 4:2.

the hidden things of dishonesty and shame, but had renounced them. Their conduct was not in craftiness or subtlety, nor did they handle the Word of God deceitfully. They did not take a theological position and manipulate the Word of God to make it fit that stance. Paul exhorted young Timothy to be *a workman that needeth not to be ashamed, rightly dividing the word of truth.*[1] It is very easy to take the Word of God and handle it with some ulterior motive. Satan himself used the Word of God in this way when he tempted Jesus in the wilderness. He wrested precious truth and took it out of its context.

How should we regard other people's consciences?

In this matter of openness perhaps the most important declaration of the apostle Paul is that we should by manifestation of the truth commend ourselves to every conscience of men before God.

This word manifestation literally means 'open show' and 'display'. What is on display is truth in every sense of that word. Please note that this manifestation of truth is commended to every conscience of men. People reared in various traditions sometimes have different consciences about certain ethical matters. Our attitude to the Sabbath, for example, is an emotive subject of conscience in some circles. What really matters is that we do not run away or hide from people because they have different ways or views. We commend ourselves to every conscience of men.

When the Lord sent me first to America and Canada, then later to South Africa, it was very liberating to know that I could commend myself to every conscience of men and accept people for who and what they were regardless of their differing traditions, cultures and backgrounds. I did not necessarily agree with their traditions, and in some cases I may have felt that the way their consciences interpreted the things of God was

[1] 2 Tim. 2:15.

incorrect. In such openness, however, the Lord gave largeness of heart and understanding, reminding us that perhaps some of our traditions were not wholly right before the Lord.

We have to be willing to learn and submit to others in the fear of God. We have to be absolutely open and honest, for otherwise we build up barriers in our mind that mar the fellowship that the Holy Spirit is seeking to bring in the Body of Christ.

Openness of heart does not mean compromise. If God has given us a conscience about certain things which differs from the consciences of others let us be faithful to it. But to impose it on others as a basis for fellowship could well be wrong, and may divide and fragment the beautiful thing that God is doing. Later we shall be looking at respect for one another.

'Walking in the light' sessions

In this matter of walking in the light, as in everything else, there are areas we should seek to safeguard. We can become unbalanced and take this, like everything else, to extremes. Certain practices have been brought to my notice in the last few years to which we should give special attention.

Some groups of people have 'light sessions' in the church. Pastors or other leaders of the flock interrogate the members, sometimes in a group, sometimes individually. The degree of openness demanded is that to which all the unwholesome past life is exposed to view. Often things that have already been confessed to God and forgiven by the grace of our Lord Jesus are included in this exposure. This can be very dangerous, for although the intention is to create honesty and provide healing and cleansing in those areas that were ill affected in one's life, the end is often a guilt complex; the bondage of living under a cloud of condemnation and humiliation through unjustifiable exposure before other people. This can be a stratagem of the evil one to bring people into bondage and fear.

Confession of sin

Another danger in the realm of openness is when private and secret sin in certain people's lives is revealed purportedly under the operation of the gifts of the Spirit. The leader calls for a public confession from the individual or persons concerned. Unsympathetic spectators in this public situation observe the exposure and the devil is given ground to exploit the fellowship by dragging it through the mud.[1]

Open confession in a prayer group

I have discovered another very subtle trend in some of today's cell and prayer groups. It is taught that, to be effective in prayer, there must be perfect agreement and accord. Openness is called for and any unconfessed sin or uncleanness in the life is expected to be exposed before the others gathered together. Faults and failings are aired publicly and prayer is made for forgiveness and cleansing. This sounds good, but I have personally witnessed a lot of harm come from this practice. Some in the group may be mature enough to cope with such exposure, while other less mature members do not know how to react wisely. The individual who makes the confession feels exposed but submits to it in all sincerity.

True love does not expose the faults of others. Love covers a multitude of sins and does not wilfully expose them.[2] Jesus gave clear instruction concerning such matters. *Moreover if thy brother shall trespass against thee, go and tell him his fault between thee and him alone: if he shall hear thee, thou hast gained thy brother.*[3] There is no suggestion here of open exposure at this stage. Only the two parties concerned are involved. It is only when there is a lack of response to this procedure that scripture allows for open exposure of the kind mentioned.

[1] See 'War on the Saints', J. Penn-Lewis, CLC (USA), 1977, Ed. P. 75.

[2] 1 Peter 4:8. [3] Matt. 18:15-17.

Openness in money matters

A very emotive subject calling for thorough openness is that of finance. There should never be a single thing to hide when it comes to money matters in the kingdom of God. The sin of Ananias and Sapphira, so promptly dealt with in the early church, was that of deception in the matter of finance.[1]

It appears that only in one instance in scripture were tithes paid to an individual, i.e. when Abram paid tithes to Melchizedek at the time of the slaughter of the kings.[2] Later the Lord commanded through the prophet—*Bring ye all the tithes into the storehouse.*[3]

Scripture clearly permits the servants of God to receive money from the Lord's people towards their support, for *they who preach the gospel should live of the gospel.*[4] All such servants should be publicly known for their trustworthiness. It is an honour to be entrusted by the Lord with the stewardship of such funds. A cause of deep concern, is the existence of questionable practices in financial matters amongst the Lord's people. It is imperative that there should be total openness in the handling of the Lord's money. In a fellowship it is wise to ensure that personnel, other than those who are recipients of the funds, have the responsibility of the stewardship of such money.[5]

It should go without saying that in this regard both individuals and fellowships who are in receipt of financial support from the Lord's people should be accountable. Independently audited accounts should always be available, and the impression that there is something to hide should never be permitted to develop.

In this ministry on openness as an expression of true submission in the fear of God, there are clear guide lines in God's Word. God wants His people to get things together on a right basis and in balance. If we are going to see true unity within our assemblies and among all our fellowships there has to be openness and honesty of heart, but in accordance with the teaching of God's Word.

[1] Acts 5:1-11. [2] Gen. 14:20. [3] Mal. 3:10. [4] 1 Cor. 9:14. [5] 1 Cor. 16:3, 4.

Openness at leadership level

May the day soon dawn when Spirit-filled leaders, currently working in separate fields of service within largely man-made denominational and organisational structures, will recognise that the potential of ministry within them is necessary, not only within the confines of their establishments, but also to other members of the Body of Christ. Leaders should be able to communicate together and discover in each other what the area and nature of that leadership is. Ministries of apostles, prophets, evangelists, pastors and teachers are needed now in the Body. Some of them are already in existence but are often confined to certain sects and groups.

There must come openness and open-facedness at leadership level. How can the members of local bodies ever come together if there is no communication between their leaders? Conference, consultation, sharing and openness at leadership level are vital. In such an atmosphere, grace and the wisdom of the Spirit of God should abound, so that there will be no lack of spiritual guidance and every necessary ministry for the members of the Body of Christ.

Openness between members of the Body of Christ

There should be openness of heart between all the members of a flock. They should also feel free to share their burdens, their problems, even their weaknesses and failures with their oversight. In the fuller setting of the Body of Christ members of different fellowships should find an openness in sharing their faith and love.

We need, as different fellowships, to be exposed to one another in ways which we have not been used to. In each God-anointed fellowship there are ministries that the rest of the Body needs. God is going to bring His people together in openness because we need each other more than we realise.

Due to fear and a lack of openness with each other, people are scared to interrelate in fellowship and therefore refuse to move across the barriers that divide them. There are fears on account of disloyalty or unfaithfulness. Such things should be banished from our minds. We should all know where God has set us and there should be no question about our loyalty and faithfulness there. Yet, we should be able to relate together openly in the wider context of the Body of Christ, and sense the warmth of fellowship and oneness of Spirit.

7

Respect

Let us not therefore judge one another any more: but judge this rather, that no man put a stumblingblock or an occasion to fall in his brother's way. . . . Let us therefore follow after the things which make for peace, and things wherewith one may edify another. . . . Hast thou faith? have it to thyself before God. Happy is he that condemneth not himself in that thing which he alloweth.[1]

Coping with various traditions

To submit to one another means that we have a respect for one another. We all have different backgrounds and traditions and Paul emphasises this when he deals with such questions as eating, drinking, judging the stewardship of other people, special days, and so on. We all differ to some degree in our consciences about the things we can allow and disallow. When we come together however, we have to respect each other, particularly when there are so many extremes of tradition, thinking and practice. Paul is very clear on this.

One man's conscience will interpret scriptural guide lines differently from another depending on social, family and denominational background. We should be aware of this as we begin to open up to those in other walks of life or branches of the Christian Church. Our Christian consciences are conditioned by such influences as prevailing traditions; the interpretation of legalism and freedom within our fellowships, the nature of

[1] Romans 14:13, 19, 22.

teaching in such matters as grace, the sacraments, Church discipline, etc.

The Lord is far less concerned about our external observances than we are. He does not even demand uniformity in forms of worship, customs, traditions and organisations; but He is concerned about the unity of the Spirit. Some of these things are so superficial and irrelevant that we must see past them if we are to experience the glory of the Lord in our land. People should be enjoying the Lord: knowing and experiencing kingdom life, which is *righteousness and peace and joy in the Holy Ghost.*[1]

Jerusalem and Antioch

The Jerusalem Church was very different from the new Antioch Christian Centre but God blessed both mightily. The problems arose only when one tried to impose its traditions on the other. It was then that hypocrisy, pride, division and legalism began to evidence themselves in the early Church. This experience, and later similar incidents, prompted Paul to write about these matters and plead for mutual respect.

Judging others

We are prohibited by Scripture from judging fellow believers on the basis of their behaviour or our interpretation of what is right and wrong concerning external observances. We are told to respect one another for our different convictions. In this regard we have to look into our brother's or sister's face and say "my brother (or sister), I think differently from you, but I respect you. I hope you respect me. My conviction is equally as important to me as yours is to you, but please let us respect each other."

If I am walking in the light with an open heart before God and am fully accepted by Him, why should I then be subject to the judgment of man? The only one we should judge, says Paul, is ourself. We must ensure that our behaviour does not cause a

[1] Romans 14:17.

brother or sister to stumble or fall.

Head-covering

Let us briefly consider the matter of women wearing head coverings during public worship. For some this is a critical subject and brings them into a real crisis of conscience. There are those who feel that the Scripture makes a clear statement on this requirement. Others believe that the teaching has to be interpreted in the light of eastern culture. Paul's teaching on such observances is clear. If one believes that such a practice is required by Scripture, then it would be sin to ignore it. Alternatively, if one's conscience is clear before God in non-compliance, then one is acting in faith. In either case, neither is permitted to judge or despise the other.

Unless we can come to terms with matters like this we shall remain divided. God wants us to love one another, even if we have a different approach to such things. What is important is that people can enjoy kingdom living, with righteousness and peace and joy in the Holy Ghost, without having to make disproportionate emphases on external observances.

We are going to have to meet this generation the way that Jesus met his generation, by putting the emphasis on matters of the heart. In a situation where it would be considered offensive for women not to wear head coverings, we should be careful not to cause offence. The sisters should wear a covering without any feeling of being in bondage, dictated to or imposed upon. We should have respect for those who feel deeply about it.

Unclean meats

I know, and am persuaded by the Lord Jesus, that there is nothing unclean of itself; but to him that esteemeth any thing to be unclean, to him it is unclean. But if thy brother be grieved with thy meat, now walkest thou not charitably.[1] How should we

[1] Romans 14:14.

react and how should we judge in the matter of clean and unclean meats according to Old Testament law? This, says Paul, should be resolved on the basis of love.

Here was a delicate issue for those with a Judaistic background. For those with pagan backgrounds, as in Asia Minor and Europe, the issue was of meat that had been offered to idols. If we were to place traditionally forbidden meat before such a person and say "I am not bound by such legalistic bondages" Paul would say *Now walkest thou not charitably.*

Necessity of love and peace

We must relate to and judge one another on the basis of love. If we discover that our practices cause offence or cause a brother or sister to stumble then it is our responsibility to respect them and do that which is charitable. Jesus said *By this shall all men know that ye are my disciples, if ye have love one to another.*[1] We must consider one another in love, and by love serve one another.

Our judgment in such situations must also be on the basis of peace. *Let us therefore follow after the things which make for peace, and things wherewith one may edify another.*[2] We should examine our attitudes to our brothers and sisters in the light of this command, even when their views relating to form, order, observance or tradition differ from ours. Let the peace of God rule in our hearts and let our brothers and sisters feel God's peace flowing out from us: *For the kingdom of God is not meat and drink (or external observances); but righteousness, and peace, and joy in the Holy Ghost.*[3]

It has been a most illuminating experience for me to be sent by the Lord to other countries and meet so many believers from a variety of cultures and background. I have found freedom to meet people from differing traditions who think and act differently from those whom I normally encounter, yet whose

[1] John 13:35. [2] Romans 14:19. [3] Romans 14:17.

dedication, love for God and prayer life are just as zealous. We should thank God for all brothers and sisters regardless of race, colour, culture or background and be prepared to identify with them at their level of experience in an atmosphere of mutual respect.

Getting together

With this attitude we will experience the kinship of spiritual fellowship immediately. The barriers that exist in our minds will vanish. We shall be united by the Spirit of God and the kingdom of God will truly be righteousness and peace and joy in the Holy Ghost. It is the Holy Spirit who unifies God's people. Bond or free, Jew or Gentile: we can belong to the Jerusalem Church with its traditions, or the Antioch Church with its liberty.

The Holy Spirit can unite us as He did in the council of Jerusalem when the apostles and elders of the Church came together to discuss the things that seemed to be dividing them concerning their traditions, such as the keeping of the law and circumcision. All those who had gathered from the Gentile Churches and the Jewish community with their differing traditions were . . . *assembled with one accord.*[1] Unless we come together like that we cannot know true fellowship for we are all so very different. Within the different groups many are crying out for God, yearning and longing for a move of the Spirit of God. The basis of such a move must be love, peace and mutual edification (building up of each other). Spiritual superiority or inferiority complexes should not exist among us. ''Make us one'' should be the cry of our hearts. Let us build, encourage, strengthen and bless our brothers and sisters.

Walking in the light

Our behaviour should never cause a brother or sister to stumble, or be offended or weakened in faith. It is vital then that

[1] Acts 15:25.

we consider one another in love. We should be at peace about what we allow in our brothers and sisters if we are walking in the light before God. We should also respect the convictions of others who are walking in peace, openness, light and blessing.

How blessed it is to have respect and to be respected. That is how it should be in the Christian community. Individuals are hurt and fellowship marred when there is lack of respect. All of us like to feel that we are accepted for who and what we are. God has respect for every individual soul. Sin has damaged and marred us, but God loves us so much that He sent His son amongst us to save, heal and restore us. Even when we have gone astray and His image in us has been marred by sin, rebelliousness and disobedience, He still yearns after us and seeks to restore us.

Only by the power of the Holy Spirit can we know long-suffering and patience. This is what leads to respect for each other and brings freedom from self-condemnation and the fear of the condemnation of others. We will desire to see only the glory of God in His people. Feelings of inadequacy, inferiority, guilt and non-acceptance will be removed. The compassion of Christ and His wonderful grace will flow from us. This will encourage, strengthen, bless and build up our brothers and sisters in the faith. We will apply ourselves to rightly discerning the Lord's Body and will thus relate together on the basis of love, peace and edification.

8

Love

And above all things have fervent love among yourselves: for love shall cover the multitude of sins.[1] *Let love be without dissimulation. Abhor that which is evil; cleave to that which is good.*[2] Jesus Himself said *By this shall all men know that ye are my disciples, if ye have love one to another.*[3]

Love in submission

Submission to one another includes loving one another. We cannot properly submit to those we do not love or who do not love us. When we have true faith in the Lord Jesus then there is no problem in having *love unto all the saints.*[4] Paul said we can possess all the gifts and manifestations of the Spirit, understanding all knowledge and mysteries, and even exercise mountain-moving faith, yet, without love, we are nothing. We can be philanthropic and sacrificial, but it profits nothing without love.[5]

True love does not merely dictate to people and instruct them in the way they should go, but also identifies with them, seeks to understand them; suffers with them and is kind and gentle.

Caring love

When we see a fault in a brother or sister and seek to correct it and show them the right way forward, do we ensure that they also feel the warmth of our love? They must have the assurance that our ministry to them in this area springs forth out of sincere

[1] 1 Peter 4:8. [2] Romans 12:9. [3] John 13:35. [4] Eph. 1:15. [5] 1 Cor. 13.

and fervent love for them. When the Lord graciously uses us to help rectify wrongs and put people straight, His love in us will never seek to expose them but will cover the multitude of sins.

Walking in the light does not mean that we expose one another's weaknesses, but having been honest and open with each other, we will cover one another in love. That does not mean we cover up wilful sin. Rather, we will understand the feeling of helplessness and weakness in people who have been overtaken in a fault, and will love them into repentance, restoration and holiness again.

How many of us are really assured of such love in the fellowship of God's people? How many of us, in fact, demonstrate such love? When counselling I am aware of the responsibility of bringing to a person's understanding what it is that is really hindering that person. The Holy Spirit does not permit us to gloss over sin. But when sin is exposed, confessed, and repented of, we know that God *is faithful and just to forgive us our sins, and to cleanse us from all unrighteousness.*[1] I am sure that the Lord wants us to be ruthless about sin, but those of us in a counselling ministry must be loving, gracious and kind. We have to face this generation in all its desperate need with the compassion of Christ, and unless our ministry is immersed in love we will never cope.

Genuine love

Let love be without dissimulation. The word simply means hypocrisy. We can say sentimentally how much we love each other, but sometimes this can be so hypocritical. God wants to deal with that. We have a problem if we are simply wearing a love-mask and parading a love-facade. We are instructed in the Word of God to love fervently and without hypocrisy. This too is the work of the Holy Spirit. *Because the love of God is shed abroad in our hearts by the Holy Ghost which is given unto us.*[2]

[1] 1 John 1:9. [2] Romans 5:5.

This love is at the heart of all Christian fellowship. In Ephesians these two little words 'en agape' [1]—in love—deal with all aspects of the Church's life. Its members walk together worthily of their vocation, but only 'in love'. They grow up together into Christ the Head, but only 'in love'. They function together causing the whole Body to be edified, but only 'in love'.

Forgiving love

Brethren, if a man be overtaken in a fault, ye which are spiritual, restore such an one in the spirit of meekness. . . . Bear ye one another's burdens, and so fulfil the law of Christ. [2] What is the law of Christ? *A new commandment I give unto you, that ye love one another; as I have loved you, that ye also love one another.* [3]

The love of Christ is a forgiving love. It is almost impossible to relate together without some offence, hurt, misunderstanding or such like arising to disturb fellowship. Provided there is no ulterior motive, love will prevail in a constant spirit of forgiveness. It was from the Cross that love cried out *Father forgive them.*

In submitting to one another it is imperative that we submit to the Cross experience. With our Lord, we have been crucified. [4] Now our life is His life in us and we are filled with His selfless love. It is Calvary love that cries *Forgive,* and the only love that truly can. In the coming together of the members of the Body we will be able to submit and adjust to one another only as we unceasingly love with the grace of forgiveness.

Impartial love.

Sadly, in my travels, I have also discovered some distortion of the *love* theme. A most grieving one is the implication that we love those closest to us in our particular 'cell' or 'commitment group' in a dimension, and with an intensity impossible with

[1] Eph. 4:2, 15, 16. [2] Gal. 6:1, 2. [3] John 13:34. [4] Gal. 2:20.

others. Whilst we can, in some measure understand the logic behind this, it does not have the pure ring of the Word of God about it.

What was important to the apostle Paul when he received news of the Ephesian saints was their *faith in the Lord Jesus, and love unto* **all the saints.** Such was the nature of the love that God had wrought in Paul in his calling and commission as the apostle to the Gentiles, that he experienced a total crucifixion of all he had held dear in his past, i.e. Judaism and Phariseeism. Right there, imprisoned in Rome, he finds himself on his knees in intercession for all the saints.

What is he praying for on their (and our) behalf? In the light of the work of the Cross in his own experience he is crying to God the Father that all will experience the inner strengthening of the Holy Spirit; the indwelling of Christ by faith; a rooting and grounding in love, and that **together—all the saints** will grasp experientially the length, breadth, depth and height of the knowledge-surpassing love of God.[1]

This is divine love: unbounded by mere human limitations; unfettered by carnal attitudes and desires; untrammelled by prejudices and partiality; unsullied with self-centredness or self-gratification. It comes from that pure river of the water of life, clear as crystal, flowing from the Throne of God and of the Lamb.

What is the practical outworking of this love in our experience? It defies imagination and supersedes all logic and reason, for it is the work of the Holy Spirit alone. *Now unto him that is able to do exceeding abundantly above all that we ask or think, according to* **the power that worketh in us.** *Unto him be glory in the church by Christ Jesus throughout all ages, world without end. Amen.*[2]

---

[1] Eph. 3:14-19. [2] Eph. 3:20, 21.

9

Trust

For God is my record, how greatly I long after you all in the bowels of Jesus Christ. . . . Being filled with the fruits of righteousness, which are by Jesus Christ, unto the glory and praise of God. . . . Only let your conversation be as it becometh the gospel of Christ: that whether I come and see you, or else be absent, I may hear of your affairs, that ye stand fast in one spirit, with one mind striving together for the faith of the gospel.[1]

If there be therefore any consolation in Christ, if any comfort of love, if any fellowship of the Spirit, if any bowels of mercies. Fulfil ye my joy, that ye be likeminded, having the same love, being of one accord, of one mind. Let nothing be done through strife or vainglory; but in lowliness of mind let each esteem others better than themselves. Look not every man on his own things, but every man also on the things of others.[2] [3]

By now we will surely understand that 'submission' does not mean that we have to subject ourselves to some dominating individuals who dictate how we should live, and what we should do at every cut and turn of our lives. Such a concept is unscriptural, unwholesome and unbalanced. New Testament submission was never intended to rob us of our own minds.

Even God does not treat us like that. He respects His image in us. What grieves the heart of God more than anything is that the image, the likeness of Himself in us, has been marred by sin. Thank God that in Christ this is being restored. The purpose of

[1] Phil. 1:8, 11, 27. [2] Phil. 2:1-4. [3] Read also Phil. 2:19-30.

God is that we might be conformed to the image of His Son. This will never destroy the sense of responsibility that we each have as individuals, nor further impair the image that has already been so marred by sin, rebelliousness and wilfulness. God is restoring His people to the likeness of their Maker and Redeemer, His blessed Son. His object is to restore us to be responsible sons of God, reflecting His glory, with whom He can relate and in whom He can delight.

Commitment demands trust

Thus, when we submit to one another in the fear of God, we will be able to trust one another. How important it is to be able to trust each other. Jesus felt strongly about this. John in his Gospel records how many people jumped on the band wagon when he performed many mighty miracles. He said *Many believed in his name, when they saw the miracles which he did. But Jesus did not commit himself unto them . . . for he knew what was in man.*[1] We need to be able to trust each other not only when we are in the midst of revival, but when the going is tough.

Trust is something that must spring forth from our relationship with the Lord. Our commitment must be first to Him. He has no problem committing Himself to us when we willingly respond to His love and allow His grace to operate in our lives.

O the wonder of His Grace! Is it not truly amazing that He chooses you and me, that He deposits in our lives the gifts of His grace? Is this not God committing Himself to us? Do we really appreciate what God has wrought in our lives? It should humble us when we realise how the grace of God has laid hold upon us. God so trusts what His grace has made of us, that He lavishes His gifts upon us and makes us stewards of His holy resources.

I pray that all of us will begin to feel anew our sense of responsibility in this. If God can trust us with the deposit of His

[1] John 2:23-25.

grace and with a stewardship of holy things for the Body of Christ then we should be able to trust one another. I recall one minister saying to me "Brother, it is not enough to talk about unity. It is as important to talk about loyalty." How loyal are we to God? We may expect that same degree of loyalty to be displayed one to another.

Some of us have learned through bitter experience the importance of being able to trust each other. How precious it is to be able to trust one another anywhere and everywhere, and to speak only commendable things of each other. Where such trust exists, if it becomes necessary to admonish one another, the initial feeling of being wounded is quickly replaced by the comforting realisation that *faithful are the wounds of a friend.*[1] And no unity in the purpose of God can ever be accomplished without this sense of trust and loyalty.

There were people to whom Jesus did commit Himself. He committed Himself to His disciples, one of whom eventually betrayed Him. They were all equally as weak in the flesh as we are without the Spirit and the grace of God. In the flesh we are prone to disloyalty and untrustworthiness, but in the Spirit and the anointing, by the deposit of His marvellous grace within us, we can be loyal to God and to one another.

Maturity discerns trust

There was a time when I used to trust people with a naive simplicity. I trusted them and did not expect that they would speak derogatorily of me in my absence. I believed that if they had any criticism of me they would confront me with it privately. I had to learn through bitter experience how important it is to be spiritually discerning. When there is a break in trust, spiritual fellowship is broken and the Spirit of God is grieved.

We are learning together that, while love thinks no evil, it does not become so spiritually naive that it does not discern evil. We

[1] Prov. 27:6.

are clearly taught that *the Word of God is quick, and powerful, and sharper than any twoedged sword, piercing even to the dividing asunder of soul and spirit . . . and is a discerner of the thoughts and intents of the heart.*[1] As God's people abide in Christ and His Word abides in them, they will yet relate in the way God purposed, for they will mature in the things of the Spirit and mutual trust will be restored.[2]

There must be no ground for mistrust. We should be able to say what we mean, and mean what we say. The idea should not be prevalent in our minds that a fellow member has some impure motive in the things that he does or says. When conversing with each other we should be assured that we have nothing but pure intentions; that the intents of our hearts and our motives are transparently sincere. Surely that is what is meant by the Psalm *Who shall ascend the hill of the Lord? or who shall stand in his holy place? He that hath clean hands, and a pure heart.*[3] He, whose heart is pure in motive, attitude and intention before God and man, ascends the hill of the purpose, presence and power of God. Only those with clean hands and pure hearts before God and one another will advance in God's purposes in the days ahead. Mutual trust is implicit if we are going to enjoy the unity of the Spirit.

[1] Hebrews 4:12. [2] John 15:1-8. [3] Psalm 24.

10

Care

I have no man likeminded, who will naturally care for your state. For all seek their own, not the things which are Jesus Christ's.[1] For our comely parts have no need: but God hath tempered the body together, having given more abundant honour to that part which lacked: That there should be no schism in the body; but that the members should have the same care one for another.[2]

The apostle Paul had a great burden of care for the Church, and he referred to Timothy, his own son in the faith, as being likeminded *who will naturally care for your state.[3]* This is the spirit of those who are submitted to one another in the Body of Christ. God sets the members in the Body as it pleases Him, because He wants that Body to function in wholeness and co-ordination. Wholeness comes not as we pull down one another, but as we minister to and care for each other.

Those who have responsibility in leadership should be able to bring correction to members of the flock when required, never out of a spirit of condemnation, but because they care. Any father who does not correct and discipline his child is lacking in love. If he really loves and cares for his child he will discipline and correct him.

To correct one another out of a spirit of caring for one another is most precious, for we desire only good for each other. Every member should be properly nourished and cared for. This is the burden of Paul's ministry concerning the Breaking of

[1] Phil. 2:20, 21. [2] 1 Cor. 12:24, 25. [3] 2 Cor. 11:28.

Bread. To discern the Lord's body aright is to recognise that we are members together in the one Body of Christ. When self is crucified and we think more about each other than about ourselves, and seek each other's good in love, no one will feel uncared for, rejected or misunderstood.

For this cause many are weak and sickly among you, and many sleep.[1] Why? Is it because they have personally sinned and done some terrible wrong in the sight of a holy God and have not confessed? It may be so, but not necessarily. The condemnation is if we, as members in the Body, do not rightly discern the Lord's Body. *For we being many are one bread, and one body; for we are all partakers of that one bread.*[2]

According to the context the unworthiness, and hence the condemnation, spring from self, pride, heresy, divisions, sectarianism, and all kinds of fleshly attitudes and behaviour which adversely affect other members.[3] This kind of coming together cannot be considered to be eating the Lord's Supper, says the apostle Paul. The revelation that I have received is of the whole Body coming together and everyone waiting for the other: being concerned one for another, so that no member of the Body will feel uncared for, rejected, forsaken, disowned. How demoralising and distressing it is to feel unloved.

Many precious believers have to suffer this. They sit in congregations and feel totally neglected, rejected and forlorn, just like a little island in a sea of humanity, totally alone and deserted. Should it ever be like that for anybody in the Body of Christ? Never. The whole concept of the Lord's table is our Christian fellowship, a concept which we should appreciate more than anything else in our Christian experience. The Greek word for *communion,*[4] twice used with regard to the Lord's table, literally means *fellowship.* It is the time when we should reflect on the unity of the whole Body and the mutual care we have and show for one another.

[1] 1 Cor. 11:30. [2] 1 Cor. 10:17. [3] 1 Cor. 11:17-22. [4] 1 Cor. 10:16—koinōnia.

So in our care we show that we are submitting to each other in the fear of God. We commit to our brothers and sisters our help, love, understanding, patience; all that God has imparted to us by His Spirit and in His marvellous grace. Such care must be both given and received by all members of the Body. Leaders and flock alike are to be strengthened and comforted by the mutual faith of each other. Otherwise members will ultimately become weak and sickly, and some may even die spiritually and physically. Even the caring apostle Paul appreciated the care of the Philippian saints for him.[1]

[1] Phil. 4:10.

11

Service

By love serve one another.[1] *Ourselves your servants for Jesus' sake.*[2]

How many of us in 'full time ministry' have said at some time in our life "I am the servant of the Lord. I am not serving man." However spiritual this may sound, it is not the language of Jesus who said *the Son of man came not to be ministered unto, but to minister, and to give his life a ransom for many.*[3]

At the last passover before the crucifixion of our Lord, He laid aside His garments and girded Himself with a towel and said *If I then, your Lord and Master, have washed your feet; ye also ought to wash one another's feet.*[4] This is the spirit of all who bear the responsibility of leadership in His Name. The apostle Paul described his own ministry similarly *We preach not ourselves, but Christ Jesus the Lord; and ourselves your servants for Jesus' sake.*[2] Every one in whom Christ dwells has the spirit of the Master who expresses His Lordship in humility, who came not to be served but to serve.

The concept of being indwelt by the Holy Spirit is concerned chiefly with relationships in the Body. The fruit of the Spirit: love, joy, peace, longsuffering, gentleness, meekness, faith, self-control: is the very life and nature of Jesus wrought in us by the Spirit, and displayed in every area of our fellowship together. How can we help but serve one another?

The fruit of the Spirit is not merely a personal possession indicative of one's spirituality. Once the Galatian believers

[1] Gal. 5:13. [2] 2 Cor. 4:5. [3] Mark 10:45. [4] John 13:14:

moved out of the life of the Spirit and endeavoured to continue in the flesh, serious relationship problems arose among them. So Paul appealed for a return to the liberty in Christ by the Spirit so that all works of the flesh would be banished and that, by love, they would again serve one another.

All responsible leaders in the service of the Lord Jesus will reflect His nature and ministry. That is why Peter appeals to all in eldership to take the oversight of the flock of God not *as being lords over God's heritage, but being ensamples to the flock.*[1] Spiritual authority they will have, but it will be reflected in Grace, humility and servanthood. In this way the members will see and follow the example set by their leaders, and the fruit of the Spirit will be manifested in all relationships.

[1] 1 Peter 5:3.

60

12

Discipline

And we beseech you, brethren, to know them which labour among you, and are over you in the Lord, and admonish you; And to esteem them very highly in love for their work's sake. And be at peace among yourselves. Now we exhort you, brethren, warn them that are unruly, comfort the feebleminded, support the weak, be patient toward all men.[1] *Remember them which have the rule over you, who have spoken unto you the word of God: whose faith follow, considering the end of their conversation. Obey them that have the rule over you, and submit yourselves: for they watch for your souls, as they that must give account, that they may do it with joy, and not with grief: for that is unprofitable for you.*[2]

Disciples are 'disciplined'

God's people are meant to be a disciplined people. The word 'disciple' comes from the same root as 'discipline'. We should thank God for the discipline that He has purposed for His Church in this indisciplined age.

To cope with the strategy of the evil one, the whole Church must become a disciplined army. It is in this area that the Church seems most vulnerable. Because so much indiscipline prevails amongst the people of God, the enemy of our souls has little problem getting at the individual members and exploiting the areas of their weakness. The devil operates by strategy, cunning and craftiness, while the Church is often haphazard and

[1] 1 Thess. 5:12-14. [2] Heb. 13:7, 17.

careless in its approach to spiritual things such as prayer, fellowship, ministry and stewardship. Therefore its members often become a prey for the devil who oppresses, torments, divides, mars and weakens them in their faith and fellowship.

Disciplining of one another

To submit one to another means that we are relating together in true fellowship. This, in itself, is a discipline. We need to be sensitive to one another in the Spirit. In this way we become aware of error or imbalance in our lives, not merely because of individual opinions, but by the consensus of Spirit-filled members. In real fellowship there is a disciplining of our lives in an atmosphere of love.

While counselling a sister at a Conference, I discovered that she had a very deep need. She was broken down mentally, spiritually and morally and was yearning to get back to God and to be again aware of His presence in her life. For three years she had been backslidden and was at first unwilling to confess the basic cause.

Finally it became very clear why her life was in such a mess. She had withdrawn from real commitment in fellowship and had begun listening to God (as she thought) on her own. She had imagined that God was saying "Do this," and "Do that," and she just obeyed.

Certainly it is an indication of maturity that we hear God speaking to us personally. But it is also vital that we are in our proper setting in the fellowship of Spirit-filled believers for then we are less likely to be deceived. Her problem was that, in her proud isolation, there was no possibility of conferring with others and receiving confirmation by other witnesses. By not walking in the light she was not having fellowship with any others.[1] She was just doing as she pleased, going her own way, not subject to discipline, correction, guidance nor help. She was

[1] 1 John 1:7.

a perfect target for satanic deception. We need the other members of the Body if we wish to know divine discipline. God wants disciples, and a disciple is a 'disciplined one'.

Discipline by leadership

I charge thee therefore before God, and the Lord Jesus Christ, who shall judge the quick and the dead at his appearing and his kingdom; Preach the word; be instant in season, out of season; reprove, rebuke, exhort with all longsuffering and doctrine.[1]

Here, Paul charges the young pastor, Timothy. Fellowship in the Body was supremely important to Paul, and in such fellowship there will always be leaders with a responsibility to discharge. Some Christians have no desire for fellowship, nor do they believe in oversight. Many examples could be given of those who refuse to come under the discipline of God-ordained fellowship and oversight. The product of such an attitude is usually a very sad and confused Christian.

The disciples of Jesus left all to follow Him and during those three years or so they made many mistakes. But through the tuition of Jesus, and later the operation of the Holy Spirit, we see them being marvellously changed by His grace. They needed discipline and so do we. We can thank God for correction from fathers in the faith. Paul said that we have many instructors but not many fathers.[2] A real father will correct and discipline his children because he loves them.

So in the fellowship of God's people discipline is essential. Those who have been given that responsibility are required and charged by God to exercise discipline, but not to be despotic, autocratic, dictatorial, legalistic or dominating. All reproving, rebuking and exhorting must be with longsuffering and supportive teaching.

It is both unscriptural and dangerous to wilfully live our Christian life in independence and isolation. It is in relating to one another that we become conscious of flaws in our motives,

[1] 2 Tim. 4:1, 2. [2] 1 Cor. 4:15.

attitudes and behaviour. In true fellowship we experience admonition and correction from Spirit-filled fathers in the faith.

It has been said that we do not need to be in fellowship to be good Christians, and that we can be satisfied at home listening to radio and television services. This is simply not true. Christ is building His Church. Every member in that Church is in submission to others, and the whole is in submission to Christ the Head. Unless my human body functions in a similar way it becomes inefficient and sick. If all limbs and organs of my body are in their right location and fulfilling their proper function, there will be a sense of wholeness and wellbeing. We need to be thus in subjection one to the other in the Body and the whole in subjection to Him who is Head over all things to the Church. For this to operate, discipline is vital.

In the same vein Paul wrote to the Thessalonians *We beseech you, brethren, to know them which labour among you, and are over you in the Lord, and admonish you; And to esteem them very highly in love for their work's sake. And be at peace among yourselves.*[1] There is a responsibility resting on all the flock to know their true, God-ordained leaders. They will be known by their works for they *labour among them*. Their responsibility of being *over them* is only *in the Lord*.

Because of the Christlike character of their oversight their admonitions will be respected and observed and they themselves will be esteemed highly *in love*. Such headship in the Body is appreciated because it is not carnally imposed. Members of the Body feel secure and protected by the covering of such headship that reflects the nature of Him who is Head over all things to the Church.

The example of marriage

That is what headship is about in marriage. The husband is the head of the wife, not to lord it over her, nor dominate her,

[1] 1 Thess. 5:12.

but to love, cover and protect her; to enable her to become what she could not be without him. Thus she becomes beautiful and glorious just as God purposed for the Church: for *Christ also loved the church, and gave himself for it; . . . that he might present it to himself a glorious church, not having spot, or wrinkle or any such thing.*[1]

Leadership must exemplify discipline

The writer to the Hebrews says: *Remember them which have the rule over you, who have spoken unto you the word of God: whose faith follow, considering the end of their conversation. . . . Obey them that have the rule over you, and submit yourselves: for they watch for your souls, as they that must give account, that they may do it with joy, and not with grief: for that is unprofitable for you.*[2]

Here is the solemn responsibility that God in His marvellous grace has committed to leaders, giving them a stewardship of holy things. They are to nurture the flock of God in the life of the Spirit with all gravity, honour, respect, and will give account to God for them.

Humility—the hallmark of discipline

Peter exhorts all leaders and members of the flock to be *clothed with humility.* Concerning such people Paul says that their *faith follows* them. This example of godly living has a marked effect for good on the flock. When we reach that place of humility God will give us added responsibility. Only in this way can He entrust us with it, for *God resists the proud and gives grace to the humble.*[3]

Later, we shall look more closely at humility in this context, for this must be at the heart of all ministries of responsibility and authority in the Body. The hallmark of our Lord's ministry was humility. This humility is learned and displayed as we submit,

[1] Eph. 5:25-27. [2] Heb. 13:7, 17. [3] 1 Peter 5:5.

the younger to the elder, and are subject one to another. Only on this basis does God impart His grace for added responsibility and stewardship.

To meet this generation with all its fear, confusion, sin and indiscipline, the Church must be immersed in this kind of submission, with its Spirit-anointed discipline. We will reach them with the gospel in the midst of their darkness, coldness and bondage, and bring them into our company where there is openness, understanding, welcome, warmth and the love of God.

What are we to do with souls we lead to Christ? Where are they to go? What example do we set them? How are they going to learn discipline? How are they going to receive instruction? Where are they going to be nurtured and cared for?

These questions should inspire us to cease playing at Church and get together God's way. New Testament submission is not in the flesh nor bound by carnal legalism. It is in the warmth and beauty of life in the Spirit. It is vitally important that we come into a place of discipline like this, so that we can face the subtle strategy of satan, who is out to exploit indiscipline and weakness in the Body and defeat what God is doing.

God's disciplined army

We must have a clear vision of the Church, for it is not a poor, feeble company just managing to hold its own. It is a disciplined army with Jesus Christ as its captain and Lord. We cannot be defeated because Jesus said that He will build His Church and the gates of hell shall not prevail against it.[1]

The vision of God's army given to us in the Psalms shows it consisting of willing people in the day of His power; living in Christ's ascension life; reigning in His Lordship and authority in the midst of His enemies; all its members virile with youthfulness, standing shoulder to shoulder in holy array.[2] It is invincible, impregnable, disciplined and mighty through God.

[1] Matt. 16:18. [2] Psalm 110.

Indiscipline in the people of God with everyone doing as he likes, members being disjointed and fleshly attitudes towards one another, brings weakness in spiritual conflict and allows individuals to become prey for the devourer. On the other hand, being subject one to another in the fear of God, clothed with humility and standing together under His divine authority, there is strength and discipline.

His authority is not only over the Church but is vested in the Church. The Church is on the offensive, storming the gates of hell (authorities of darkness) which fall and crumble before the reigning authority of Christ as it moves forward. Though we may not have attained such an ascendancy as yet, we can believe that we are developing in that direction. The army of the Lord shall march forward.

> I am building a people of power,
> I am making a people of praise,
> That will move through this land by My Spirit,
> And will glorify My precious Name.
> Build your Church Lord, make it strong Lord,
> Join our hearts Lord through your Son.
> Make us one Lord, in your Body,
> In the kingdom of your Son.

In vision I see God's army marching through the land; disciplined and advancing together in holy array. The enemy is exposed and routed. The kingdom of darkness falls. The prayer that Jesus taught us to pray coming to pass: *Thy kingdom come* (right into the impossible situations that are confronting us), *Thy will be done on earth as it is in heaven.*

The kingdom of God shall be manifest in situations where presently the kingdom of darkness prevails. Spiritism, magic, witchcraft, the occult and everything of satanic origin will be exposed for what it is. Every dominating, deceiving, devilish stratagem in the lives and minds of men and women around us will be uncovered and dealt with. People will be restored to sanity; brought to salvation and to the healing of the Lord.

God's Church will be moving in the fulness of the victorious accomplishment of our Lord Jesus.

Submitting to discipline

Jesus calls us to go into all the world and make disciples of all nations, i.e. to make 'disciplined ones'.[1] To submit to one another is to come under the discipline of real admonition, instruction and pastoral care. In other words we submit to the discipline of fellowship. It may be from other members or from those who are our overseers. But we can never discipline others until we ourselves are subject to it.

God has a disciplined army, not a company of individuals claiming exclusive personal directions from their Lord. When God speaks to us He confirms His word through other members in the Body of Christ. Thus we are preserved from those who go around doing fanatical and unbalanced things. In this way we become part of God's disciplined army, and the enemy is routed rather than God's people becoming a prey for all his subtle strategies and intrigues.

Making disciples

Making 'disciplined ones' does not mean imposing regimentation on believers. It is rather the discipline that results from the willing response of those who realise the claims of the Lord Jesus Christ in their lives. This discipline has right priorities and responds to the scriptural appeal to present our body as a living, holy sacrifice. It submits to the total Lordship of Christ; commits itself to the fellowship of the Body in the setting God has ordained for it; and is an example to the whole Church.

His disciples—or ours?

I have discovered one major problem in the area of discipleship among certain groups. There is a teaching and practice that

[1] Matt. 28:19 (literal translation).

gives the impression that people are called to be our disciples; that we are to make disciples for ourselves. What did Jesus really say about this? *All authority is given unto me in heaven and in earth. Go ye therefore, and teach all nations baptising them in the name of the Father, and of the Son, and of the Holy Ghost: Teaching them to observe all things whatsoever I have commanded you; and, lo, I am with you alway, even unto the end of the age. Amen.*[1]

The command is to disciple; to train; to teach all nations, baptising them into the Name of the Father, and the Son, and the Holy Spirit. Therefore the new life they share is divine life. They share the life of Him whose Name is called Emmanuel, God with us. Our disciplining of people is to commit people to a relationship with and in the triune God. We are called to train disciples of Jesus. He did not say that we are to teach them to observe all things we command them. He said, *teaching them to observe all things whatsoever I have commanded you.*

*Then said Jesus to those Jews which believed on him, if ye continue in my word, then are ye **My disciples** indeed, And ye shall know the truth, and the truth shall make you free.*[2] He did not even begin to suggest that they would be anybody else's disciples. Notice also the emphasis on *My disciples* in the following references. *By this shall all men know that ye are **My disciples,** if ye have love one to another.*[3] *If ye abide in me, and my words abide in you, ye shall ask what ye will, and it shall be done unto you. Herein is my Father glorified, that ye bear much fruit; so shall ye be **My disciples.***[4]

How did the apostles in the early Church apply this command of Jesus? It is quite clear that on the day of Pentecost, the day the Holy Spirit came to anoint and empower those early Church disciples, Peter instructed three thousand new converts first to repent, secondly to be baptised in the Name of the Lord Jesus, thirdly that they would receive the gift of the Holy Spirit.[5] After

[1] Matt. 28:18-20. [2] John 8:31, 32. [3] John 13:35. [4] John 15:7, 8. [5] Acts 2:37-42.

this initial response they all continued steadfastly, first in the teaching of the apostles, secondly in fellowship, thirdly in the breaking of bread, and fourthly in prayer.

The apostle Paul, describing his own ministry among the people, declared how he had instructed them in the matter of repentance toward God and faith toward our Lord Jesus Christ.[1] To the Ephesians he clearly emphasised basic beginnings of discipleship in the following terms: *After I heard of your faith in the Lord Jesus, and love unto all the saints, cease not to give thanks for you, making mention of you in my prayers; that the God of our Lord Jesus Christ, the Father of glory, may give unto you the spirit of wisdom and revelation in the knowledge of him: the eyes of your understanding being enlightened.*[2]

Their instruction in discipleship involved true commitment to the Lord. This manifested itself in love amongst all the saints so that everyone would come to know God for himself, to hear His voice and to know the purpose of God in His Church.

[1] Acts 20:21. [2] Eph. 1:15-18.

13

Edification

Whatever our ministry or exercise in the Body, whether prophesying, speaking in tongues, interpreting tongues, giving revelation or even quoting a Psalm: *Let all things be done unto edifying.*[1] The word 'edify' comes from the word 'edifice'—a building. *I will build my Church.*[2] . . . *The building fitly framed together groweth unto a holy temple in the Lord: . . . an habitation of God through the Spirit.*[3] God, who dwells in high heaven, wants it to be known that His Church is designed to be the habitation of His presence. Then will the people of this world sit up and take note that God is among His people.

Gifts of the Spirit edify

The Lord Jesus Christ is building His Church. Any building we are doing can only be of relevance if it is in accordance with His programme. *Except the Lord build the house they labour in vain that build it.*[4] It is clear from our Scripture reading that to be able to edify (or build up) the Church we need the fulness and anointing of the Holy Spirit.[1] Only then can we function in the Church, not by our own natural talents and abilities, but by the imparted gifts of the Holy Spirit.

The Word clearly teaches that these gifts are subject to our personal control, hence there is need for a very responsible approach to their exercise. It is in this context that Paul appeals: *Let everything be done unto edifying.*

[1] 1 Cor. 14:26 (Read also vv. 4, 5, 12, 16). [2] Matt. 16:18. [3] Eph. 2:21, 22. [4] Psalm 127:1.

Sharing our faith edifies

As stated, everything we do should be to build up the people of God. *Let no corrupt communication proceed out of your mouth, but that which is good to the use of edifying, that it may minister grace to the hearers.*[1] *Let us therefore follow after the things which make for peace, and things wherewith one may edify another.*[2] The forces of darkness are exploiting the spirit of criticism in the Church which is producing rivalry, party spirit, fragmentation, and is the fertile soil for the germination of seeds of self-destruction.

When we have something to say, let it be something which will build up the Church. Whilst the devil and evil men want to destroy us, the life of the Spirit in His people is intent on building us up. How we long to see all God's people built up in the faith: encouraged, strengthened and edified.

For years many of us have lived self-centred lives, caring only how we can be blessed, edified or comforted. We are needing to re-orient our thinking and be filled with a desire to help build up the Body. We should want the Lord's blessing, not from selfish motives, but that it may flow out of our lives to build up the Church. New converts, as babes in Christ, need nurturing and building up. Initially we should not expect too much from them.

Those of us who have been maturing in the life of the Spirit should now concern ourselves with building up one another in the fellowship and the Church at large. Every time we function in the gifts, speak the Word, minister to others, converse with each other, pray to God, or whatever we do, we should be thinking about edification. We should ask ourselves: Is the Church going to be built up? Are God's people going to be edified? Is my ministry, my witness, my attitude, my motive, everything that I am, everything that I do, edifying to the Church? Submitting to one another in the fear of God involves all this.

[1] Eph. 4:29. [2] Romans 14:19.

Henceforth, let everything to do with self: self-centredness, self-will, self-pity, self-projection, be crucified with Christ. *I am crucified with Christ: nevertheless I live; yet not I, but Christ liveth in me: and the life which I now live in the flesh I live by the faith of the Son of God, who loved me, and gave himself for me.*[1] Our concern is no longer for ourselves, but for others. We will seek to excel only to the edifying of the Church which is His Body.

The fulness of the Spirit edifies

We can never outgive God. The more we give the more we receive in abundance. *Give, and it shall be given unto you; good measure, pressed down, and shaken together, and running over.*[2] The purpose given by Jesus for receiving the Holy Ghost is not just that we should be filled, but that out of our innermost being should flow rivers of living water.[3] The blessing we have received is needed by others. The Body of Christ is edified by our presence and function, but since we are part of that Body, it naturally follows that our own life will in turn be enriched and built up.

God wants us built up and strong as individuals, but not independently and in isolation from one another. *For as we have many members (limbs and organs) in one body, and all members have not the same office (function); so we, being many, are one body in Christ, and every one members one of another.*[4]

In submitting we edify

Let us remember that the word submission, however much it has been distorted by man, is a beautiful word from the scriptures inspired by the Holy Spirit. We need to understand it and not fear it, then face up to its meaning in our lives and in the fellowship. We now know that in submitting to one another in the fear of God, the concept of persons in authority lording over

[1] Gal. 2:20. [2] Luke 6:38. [3] John 7:38. [4] Romans 12:4, 5.

us, demanding implicit, unquestioning obedience is not simply wrong but totally unscriptural and exceedingly dangerous. To submit to one another is to enjoy meaningful fellowship together.

This means that we are concerned about the unity of the Spirit in the Church; that we will have mutual respect for each other's consciences and convictions. Love will be at the heart of all our fellowship, and trust will develop as we increasingly exercise care for each other. In love we will render service to one another and not simply wait to be served. We will discipline and be disciplined graciously because love and grace are abounding in our hearts. We will desire only the very best for each other.

In submitting to one another we recognise that God has set the members in the Body as it has pleased Him. As the limbs and organs of my body are set and co-ordinated together for perfect functioning of the whole, so God has designed the Church, as the Body of Christ, with all the members having the same care one for another. Gone are the days when it suffices just to 'attend Church' on Sunday morning, pass the time of the day in each other's company, then go home and forget Church for another week. To submit to one another means real and practical fellowship (or koinōnia, as the original Greek text puts it), in which we share our life, our faith and our love.

14

Delegated Authority

Imposition of authority

We have been looking at the meaning of submitting one to another as members in the Body of Christ. Now we shall examine more closely the exhortation to those who are younger in the faith to recognise spiritual authority in those who are older and more mature. Peter instructs *Ye younger, submit yourselves unto the elder.*[1] In no way does this suggest that the elders impose authority upon those who are younger. Nowhere in the Word of God is authority permitted to be imposed on God's children. The imposition of legal authority deals with lawlessness but that is another matter.[2] In fact Peter prefaces his remarks to the young by instructing the elders not to be *lords over God's heritage.*[3]

Submission to authority

In submitting to one another, those who are less mature are exhorted to be submissive and respectful to those who are more mature. Those who are older in the faith, especially those who are particularly called of God to exercise leadership and the responsibility of counsel, guidance or instruction, are exhorted to do so in a fatherly and faithful manner appropriate to their calling.

[1] 1 Peter 5:5. [2] 1 Tim. 1:9.

[3] 2 Cor. 1:12-24 deals beautifully with Paul's sense of authority towards the Corinthians and states *Not that we have dominion over your faith.*

Women and authority

The apostle Paul also clearly instructs *The aged women likewise, that they be in behaviour as becometh holiness, not false accusers, not given to much wine, teachers of good things: That they may teach the young women to be sober, to love their husbands, to love their children, To be discreet, chaste, keepers at home, good, obedient to their own husbands, that the word of God be not blasphemed.*[1]

The need for authority

From the Scriptures already quoted, much has been gleaned about submitting to God-ordained authority. When this is ignored the result is often distress and failure. When there has been a need for mature wisdom, with its help, strength and comfort, younger Christians, in conceit or just plain rebellion, have sometimes gone their own way with irreversibly sad results. All should recognise authority that is God-given and which bears the anointing of the Holy Spirit.

God does not call upon anyone to exercise carnal, dictatorial and dominating authority in His Church. Nor does he expect the members of the Body ever to submit to such. Experience proves that there are sometimes problems in this area. Representatives of governing bodies, presbyteries and councils, and also individual leaders, have been known to demand unquestioning, blind submission to their authority. That is why it is vital that we examine what the Word of God has to say about authority in the Church.

Delegated authority defined

*God . . . hath put all things under his (Christ's) feet, and gave him to be Head over **all things** to the Church, which is his body, **the fulness of him** that filleth all in all.*[2]

[1] Titus 2:3-5. [2] Eph. 1:22, 23.

Since this is so, then all the authority and power of Christ's Headship are in His Body. As the Body functions in perfect co-ordination with the Head, the fulness of His Headship is clearly displayed both within and through it. The ascended Christ led captive a captive multitude and gave gifts to His Church of apostles, prophets, evangelists, pastors and teachers. These are clearly meant to reflect and demonstrate His Headship. It is essential to understand this, for, since God is a God of order and has therefore designed means of controlling all His affairs, this is no less true of His Purpose within the Church. He has delegated authority to His gifted servants.

Thus, both in Christian marriage and in Church fellowship, those who bear the responsibility of headship can only exercise authority as they themselves are submitted to Christ the Head. The only real authority they have is His, and this can only be reflected as they are submitted to Him, thus manifesting the nature of Him who is the Head.

Questions on authority

In this connection many questions still arise. What about those, for instance, who say they do not submit to man but only to God, or to Christ the Lord? In a local Church context does God expect us to submit to the oversight authority unquestioningly? Should that authority be vested in one man such as a minister, priest, pastor or shepherd? These questions are both relevant and vital, particularly in these days when so much confusion and conflict prevails in these areas, and they will be discussed later.

What is the relationship between submission and authority? To submit to authority is clearly taught in the Scriptures, for Peter says: *Ye younger, submit yourselves unto the elder.*[1] For the same reason the elders are referred to as those who have the rule,[2] and as those who have to give an account to God for the flock.[3]

[1] 1 Peter 5:4. [2] 1 Tim. 3:4. [3] Heb. 13:17.

In the same context there is reference to *governments*[1] in the Body of Christ.

Authority is for order and discipline

The teaching on authority in God's Church is very clearly scriptural. God has order in His Church. God has not called His Church out of the world to be bogged down by systems of men. But neither has God purposed that His Church should be undisciplined. Without a God-ordained leadership there would be the danger of carelessness; every man doing what is right in his own eyes, and ultimately, anarchy would prevail.

Unless we have government in the Church with order under the Headship of Christ, how ever can those of us involved in Church leadership understand how to exercise authority? Paul referring to a brother going to the civil law against another brother said: *Do you not know that the saints shall judge the world? . . . and that we shall judge angels?*[2] God expects His Church to practise government now.

God's purpose for authority

Just as Elijah was able to exercise spiritual authority in Israel, without the necessity of political strategy, so will the Church when it becomes in the nation what God has called it to be. All national and local government shall come under the influence of the authority vested in the Church of Jesus Christ.

From the Psalms we understand that the ascended Christ now rules in the midst of His enemies, and the picture is clearly portrayed that his ruling authority is through His willing people, His Church, who stand as a mighty army shoulder to shoulder in holy array.[3]

Such should be the power of the prayers of God's people and the influence of their lives in the community, that God's

[1] 1 Cor. 12:28. [2] 1 Cor. 6:1-3. [3] Psalm 110.

authority, the authority of heaven, should be seen to prevail beyond all that godless and humanistic governments devise. This should be clearly manifest in the nation as well as in the townships and communities where local government can dictate, sometimes in very corrupt ways, with the Church having to stand by often powerless and ineffective.

15

Authority Exemplified

Submission to authority in the Church presupposes the spiritual authority (mark the word 'spiritual') that is characteristic of Him who is Head of the Church. By way of explanation let us examine Paul's discussion on authority in marriage.

He says, *Wives submit yourselves unto your own husbands, as unto the Lord, for the husband is head of the wife, even as Christ is the head of the church.*[1] Then adds, *Husbands, love your wives, even as Christ also loved the church, and gave himself for it.*

Submission can now be seen in its right context. If a husband loves his wife so intently that he is prepared to sacrifice his life for her, then the wife will have no difficulty in submitting to his authority.

Why did Christ love His Church so much and give His life for it? *That he might present it to himself a glorious church.*[1] The Lord Jesus Christ is the glorious Son of God, but He desires that His Church will reflect His glory. The man, says Paul, *is the image and glory of God,*[2] and his love for his wife should have as its ultimate purpose the fulfilment of the remainder of that passage, *but the woman is the glory of the man.* In other words, husbands *ought . . . to love their wives as their own bodies.*[1]

When a husband has that kind of objective, submission by the wife becomes a joy. He bears the authority and responsibility, but exercises them in a way that will cause his wife to reflect his glory. She becomes more glorious because of the covering and

[1] Eph. 5:22-28. [2] 1 Cor. 11:7.

care he provides than would ever be possible without it. She reflects that love, grace, authority and glory wrought in her husband by the Holy Spirit.

In exactly the same way, all delegated authority in the Church, under the Headship of Jesus Christ, will be spiritual authority which will reflect the nature of Jesus, and will produce a reflection of that nature in those who submit to it. What is the nature of Jesus? *Christ also loved the church, and gave himself for it.*[1] Any authority that does not reflect this sacrificial love is disqualified and invalidated.

It is sadly true that authority in the Church has often failed to reflect the nature of Christ. Since the Church tried to do in the flesh what was begun in the Spirit, it has substituted spiritual authority with different forms of ecclesiastical and hierarchical government, often exercising merely a humanly delegated, legalistic or dictatorial authority. Thus we have fragmented into denominations, organisations and man-made institutions. Once we see the scriptural requirement for government in the Church there is always the danger of setting up such authority in the flesh. This leads to proud promotions of self, and it is not long before we have such declarations as "I am in charge here," or "What I say goes here," or "I am in authority here." We can be quite sure that such dominating, legalistic authority is not ordained by God.

In recent times there has been a re-discovery of the New Testament concepts of shepherding and discipleship which has resulted in a renewed emphasis on submission to authority. Some who have embraced these truths have designated themselves 'shepherds' and assumed authoritarian leadership of a group or groups, and demanded absolute, unquestioning submission and obedience from the group members.

There have been actual cases (rare though they may be) where members have been required to sell all their possessions and

[1] Eph. 5:22-28.

hand over the proceeds to their shepherds. I have personally had dealings with people who would not make a single decision without the permission of their leader. One lady would not go to visit her mother, whom due to circumstances she would be unable to see for another two or three years, because her pastor had refused to grant her permission when requested.

There are many dangers in this area. If we have either a carnally imposed authority or a democratically appointed one these will produce after their kind. They will either subjugate and dominate on the one hand, bringing fear and confusion to many people, or, on the other hand, will pander to the irresponsibility and weakness of careless Christians and so create schism, party spirit and factions in the Body. Those who are spiritually alert will recognise such for what they are.

Once again it is necessary to reiterate that the only real authority that any leader in the Church of Jesus Christ has is spiritual. It is God alone who makes able ministers of the new testament, and their only authority is God-given. It will reflect His authority and bear all the characteristics of the Headship of Christ.

If a man is truly an apostle, his apostleship will reflect the nature and character of Christ, who is the chief apostle. A prophet will reflect Christ's prophethood. A pastor or shepherd will reflect the nature and ministry of Him, who as *the good shepherd, giveth his life for the sheep.*[1] The only authority to which people are called to submit in the Church is that which reflects the nature of Jesus. There is no need to demand submission to that. Spiritually minded people who love the Lord and are truly committed to Him will readily and joyously submit to that kind of authority, for the prophetic promise of the Word of God is *Thy people shall be willing in the day of thy power.*[2]

[1] John 10:11. [2] Psalm 110:3.

Let us not be alarmed that the Church as we have known it seems to be declining and breaking up, for there is emerging from its ruins the true Church of Jesus Christ. Its members will not be left to their own devices, for men of God will arise as true spiritual leaders and shepherds who will reflect the nature and character of the chief shepherd. The flock will follow them as they themselves follow Christ.

Much ·is expected of such shepherds. The apostle Peter says *I warn and counsel the elders amongst you—the pastors and spiritual guides of the Church—as a fellow elder, . . . tend, nurture, guard, guide and fold—the flock of God that is (your responsibility) not by coercion or constraint but willingly; not dishonourably motivated by the advantages and profits (belonging to the office) but eagerly and cheerfully. Not (as arrogant, dictatorial and overbearing persons) domineering over those in your charge, but being examples—patterns and models of Christian living—to the flock (the congregation).*[1] Such leaders reflect the characteristics displayed by Christ, the Head of the Church.

The apostle Peter identified himself with the local God-ordained elders when he said *I also am an elder.* So, as an apostle, he implied that his apostolic authority was of the same nature; not dictatorial, legalistic or dominating, but spiritual. We have already stated that spiritual authority reflects only the authority of Christ. Otherwise it is carnal and will either be weak and irresponsible or dictatorial and dominating.

What is of the flesh will never agree with what God is doing in the Spirit. We are informed that *The flesh lusteth against the Spirit, and the Spirit against the flesh: and these are contrary the one to the other.*[2] They can never agree. Fleshly or carnal authority will either seek peace at any price, or attempt to impose itself in an authoritarian and autocratic (i.e. self rule) way. Many able and godly men have failed in this area. Compromise on one

[1] 1.Peter 5:1-4 Amplified Bible. [2] Gal. 5:17.

hand or pride on the other have brought them down, and often others with them.

As in the Galatian Church, there is danger at every level of continuing in the flesh that which was begun in the Spirit. Jesus clearly taught that *That which is born of the flesh is flesh; and that which is born of the Spirit is Spirit.*[1] If authority is exercised in a carnal way, we should not be surprised when it results in rebellion, confusion and division. *For he that soweth to his flesh shall of the flesh reap corruption; but he that soweth to the Spirit shall of the Spirit reap life everlasting.*[2]

[1] John 3:5. [2] Gal. 6:8.

16

Humility

To the elders or shepherds Peter writes, *Neither as being lords over God's heritage, but being ensamples to the flock.*[1] Effective leadership is portrayed not in issuing commands, but in setting an example. To 'lead the flock' does not suggest being elevated on a platform telling folks what they should do. It is rather a picture of being an example of what they should do, and how it should be done.

That is exactly how Jesus taught. He left us all a perfect example of His authority expressed in humility when *he . . . laid aside his garments; and took a towel, and girded himself . . . and began to wash the disciples feet.*[2] This took place just prior to His betrayal and crucifixion. The company present consisted of Judas, who was about to betray Him; Peter, who would shortly deny Him with oaths and curses; and the rest who would finally forsake Him and flee at the crucial hour. Yet He washed the feet of every one.

He said to them *Ye call me Master and Lord, and ye say well; for so I am. If I then, your Lord and Master, have washed your feet; ye also ought to wash one another's feet. For I have given you an example, that ye should do as I have done to you. Verily, verily, I say unto you, The servant is not greater than his lord, neither he that is sent greater than he that sent him. If ye know these things, happy are ye if ye do them.*[3] That is how He taught headship, in terms of love and grace. His was the only valid authority, yet He exemplified it in an act of gracious humility.

[1] 1 Peter 5:3. [2] John 13:1-17. [3] John 13:13-17.

All spiritual leaders should reflect the humility of Jesus. The apostle Paul could say *We are your servants for Jesus' sake.*[1] If a leader bears authority characterised by the nature of Jesus, in the way we have just considered, it indicates the purity, grace and love there is in his spirit towards those under his charge. In his delegated responsibility a leader will deal with all the flock in a personal and distinctive way. His attitudes and motives towards those individuals will be seen to be totally impartial, sincere, gracious and loving.

Humility is required of all

Submission is not merely a ministry enjoined only on those who are young in the faith. The command of the Word of God is *Ye younger, submit yourselves unto the elder. Yea, all of you be subject one to another, and be clothed with humility: for God resisteth the proud, and giveth grace to the humble. Humble yourselves therefore under the mighty hand of God, that he may exalt you in due time.*[2]

These are commands to all believers. It is not sufficient to ask God to humble us, for we are commanded to humble ourselves. When we realise that we are what we are only by the grace of God, then we know that we have no basis for pride. God does not ask us to do anything He has not given us the grace to perform. And in the doing of it we become more and more the recipients of His grace. For *he being . . . a doer of the word, this man shall be blessed in his deed.*[3]

When the apostle says *All of you be subject one to another and be clothed with humility,* he includes even the chief of leaders, no matter how elevated his position. I am aware of the need to qualify that statement because on one occasion I misunderstood its meaning and submitted to the immature judgment of men younger in the faith, with most unpleasant results. It does not mean this kind of subjection. Young, immature

[1] 2 Cor. 4:5. [2] 1 Peter 5:5, 6. [3] James 1:25.

Christians should not be expected to bear such a responsibility. We have an example of mutual submission when the apostles and elders came together in council at Jerusalem.[1] Clearly, wisdom for the occasion was with the apostles, but the final decisions were approved and ratified by all.

To be clothed with humility and to be subject to one another is exceedingly important. All are personally responsible for obeying the command. The only way to effectively wield authority is to submit to it. It is hardly possible to exercise responsibility over others and to give proper instructions if we are not already submitting to authority ourselves. How can leaders know what to expect from those whom they lead if they are not themselves submitting to authority?

Even the centurion understood this principle when he said to Jesus that he also was a man, not **of** authority, but **under** authority. He could say to one, *Do this,* and he did it, because he was under, and therefore represented, the authority of Rome. It is when every member in the Body functions in co-ordination and in love under the Headship of Christ that true authority in the Church is manifest. No one, whatever his office, ministry or function in the Church, can minister with spiritual authority except he be clothed with humility. Only in this way will the whole Church be a revelation of the authority and glory of Christ to the world, and to principalities and powers in the heavenlies. So will the Lord Jesus be seen to rule in His Church in the midst of His enemies.[2]

Humility is a state of mind

It is worthy of note that when Paul met with the elders of the Ephesian Church for the last time, he reflected on the more important aspects of his ministry among them and put the primary emphasis on humility: *Serving the Lord with all humility of mind.*[3] The whole of his ministry in all its expressions was the product of this attitude of mind.

[1] Acts 15. [2] Psalm 110:2. [3] Acts 20:19.

I recall the complete transformation of my own ministry just six months after my ordination into full time pastoral work in January, 1957. Feeling my need for a perfect example of a faithful minister for my own guidance at the time, I began to look at Jesus as a man amongst men. Before any other virtue, I was overwhelmed by His humility. He had left the ivory palaces of glory in the incarnation, and I beheld Him facing the motley, sinful crowd at Jordan's banks. There, in dedication to His public ministry, He was baptised and literally *numbered with the transgressors.*[1] Three and a half years later he **humbled Himself** to the death of the cross. Of His own volition, He sacrificed Himself. I saw many other important attributes, such as identification with the people, determination and conviction concerning the righteousness of God being fulfilled. But humility of mind was the primary one.

The only way in which we can bear His authority is by following the Master's example. In this way we will humble ourselves under the mighty hand of God, as Jesus did. This will be our state of mind—*Let this mind be in you, which was also in Christ Jesus . . . who humbled Himself.*[2] Already the apostle Paul had experienced conflict with other ministering brethren as he records: *Some indeed preach Christ even of envy and strife; and some also of good will: The one preach Christ of contention, not sincerely, supposing to add affliction to my bonds.*[3] With this in mind he appeals to the saints at Philippi to have within them the mind of Christ: a mind of humility and meekness.

Humility is essential to true authority

Humility does not mean weakness. Neither does it express itself in false modesty, nor detract from true apostolic authority. It is the basic essential requirement for the realisation and expression of spiritual authority. To be proud is to be disqualified from bearing responsibility and authority in God's

[1] Isaiah 53:12. [2] Phil. 2:5-8. [3] Phil. 1:14-16.

service. *For God resisteth the proud, and giveth grace to the humble.*[1] There is no ability nor authority except it be given of God.

To the Corinthians, Paul, describing his ministry says: *And such trust have we through Christ to God-ward: Not that we are sufficient of ourselves to think any thing as of ourselves; but our sufficiency is of God; Who also hath made us able ministers of the new testament; not of the letter, but of the spirit; for the letter killeth, but the spirit giveth life.*[2]

We have no ability of our own. We have nothing that we have not received. We can do nothing in God's service except when He imparts the enablement by His Spirit. We have nothing outside of grace of which we can boast, so there is no justification whatsoever for pride. God resists the proud and will have *no flesh to glory in His presence.*[3] If we are not humble before God, pride will invalidate any spiritual authority we are meant to have, and we will be spiritually immobilised. In such circumstances, any authority exercised can only be carnally imposed.

Had the apostle Paul ministered in the flesh he would have ministered only a dead letter of legalism and binding dictatorial authority. Ministering the mere letter of the word without the Spirit kills, says Paul, and is but a ministry of death. Only what is ministered in the power, authority and anointing of the Holy Spirit imparts divine life to the people. It is only as we move and walk in the dimension of the Spirit of God that we will remain humble and be equipped to bear true authority. Spiritual authority has all the evidence of the fruit of the Spirit. It portrays the humility that is the primary characteristic of the chief apostle, our Lord Jesus Christ.

Humility comes from unconditional dedication

Humility is a quality of spiritual life that is produced by the unconditional dedication of the believer to God. The apostle

[1] 1 Peter 5:5. [2] 2 Cor. 3:4-6. [3] 1 Cor. 1:29.

Paul puts it very beautifully when, having appealed to the believers to present their bodies a living sacrifice to God and to be transformed by the renewing of their mind, he issues a directive with the words: *For I say, through the grace given unto me, to every man that is among you, not to think. . . .*[1]

What Paul was saying was that the only way he could exercise authority effectively in the Church was as he recognised that it was all of grace: *the grace given unto me.* Once we realise that any ability we have in ministering is not the result of mere human effort or personal attainment, but rather that *each one has received **grace** according to the measure of the gift of Christ.*[2] This understanding will ensure that we walk humbly and see to it that all we do rebounds to the Glory of His Grace alone.

Humility reflects the Glory of God's Grace

We have just seen that the appeal of the apostle Paul was on the basis of God's grace: *I say through the grace given.* It was this grace that enabled him to accept himself for what he was before God. After having seen himself as he was outside of the grace of God; not meet to be called an apostle and the chief of sinners: he says *But by the grace of God I am what I am: and his grace which was bestowed upon me was not in vain; but I laboured more abundantly than they all: yet not I, but the grace of God which was with me.*[3]

There is no indication of pride here. Neither is there any suggestion of false modesty concerning his standing and apostolic vocation in the sight of God. Both are his on account of the grace of God alone.

To denigrate ourselves and understate the work of grace in our lives, thus deceiving ourselves and others with the idea that we are something less than what God has made us, is not true humility. Someone has called it 'worm pride'. It is a false concept of humility and brings no glory to God but simply draws

[1] Rom. 12:3. [2] Eph. 4:7. [3] 1 Cor. 15:10.

attention to ourselves. There is a glory about the grace of God which should be manifest in the lives of all believers.

True humility simply accepts who and what we are by his wonderful grace. Many people are not content with themselves and would like to be other than what they are. They sometimes seek to be as other people, and to do what others do. Oh what struggles, strains and tensions result from this! True humility appreciates what God has made us, and particularly what His grace has wrought in us, enabling us to fulfil our calling.

In the service of God, pride of any description is actually a barrier against what God purposes to do in us. Pride disqualifies us because it operates outside the realm of God's grace, and endeavours to portray us as something above or below what we really are.

Humility is essential to faithful stewardship

A servant of God bears authority only as he operates in the realm of the grace of God. Outside of that grace he will either become proud, dominating, dictatorial, legalistic, demanding and even possessive, or he may be weak, compromising, careless and indifferent. In either case he is an unfaithful steward.

Whatever stewardship has been appointed to a servant of God; whether financial, material or spiritual; that stewardship can only be properly executed in the realm of the grace of God. Otherwise the result will be division, strife and tensions, and ground will be given for the manifestation of the works of the flesh, which the evil one is always on the alert to exploit.

God does not expect any believer to submit to carnal authority. Servants of Christ should never be guilty of lording it over God's heritage. They are at all times to be examples, models and patterns of Christian living, bearing forth the nature of the Lord Jesus Christ among His people. Such men and women of God will carry spiritual authority that is discernible both by men and devils. Upon such the Spirit of God rests. Christ Himself is manifested in them and through them as Lord, and the glory of God is always portrayed.

17

The Church in the Community

There is a deep concern in many hearts concerning the kind of impact that the Church has in the community. We sometimes wonder about both the individual and corporate effect of its members on the people within its sphere of influence. In the community we have to live and work among the people the way that Jesus did. In our corporate testimony we are called to portray the living Christ in His fulness to this world. This is why Jesus prayed: *That they all may be one . . . that the world may believe that thou hast sent me.*[1] The world has yet to see Christ in all His glorious fulness in the Church.

Setting of members

There should be no problem with finding our proper place in fellowship. If we are truly joined to Christ the Head, then under His Headship we will know our rightful setting in the Body: *For God sets the members in the Body as it hath pleased him.*[2] It is essential that we know and understand our setting so that we may function faithfully and loyally there, for in the living Body of Christ there are no non-functioning members.

In previous chapters we saw that every limb and organ in the human body requires the co-ordinated function of every other. Similarly, we noted that in the Body of Christ we are to be fitly joined together and compacted by that which every joint and member in the Body supplies, thus producing increase and maturity in the Body.

[1] John 17:21. [2] 1 Cor. 12:18.

Individual members living and working in the community, whether in hospitals, factories, shops, schools, colleges, offices, or simply in their neighbourhoods, reflect the life and strength they derive from such fellowship with the Lord and each other. The warmth and love in such an atmosphere causes the membership to be built up, not only in faith and maturity, but also numerically. Many will then be brought from darkness to light and will fall at the feet of Jesus. The community will become aware that God is alive among His people. The fear of God will return to our nation, and it will be recognised that Christian believers are no longer playing at Church.

Uniformity or Unity

What is the Church in the community? This can be a problem, for everywhere believers are all so different and represent such a variety of denominations which emphasise so many different doctrines, and sometimes even overtly oppose one another.

What is the Bible concept of the local Church? As far as God's Word is concerned the local Church is the company of believers in a particular location. They know that they are born again and they seek to live their lives in the fulness and power of the Holy Spirit. Each one knows what it is to have fellowship with the Father, and with His Son Jesus Christ.[1] They walk in the light as He is in the light, having fellowship one with another and experiencing the continual cleansing power of the blood of Jesus Christ.

From our fragmented historical background, we have inherited a legacy of different forms and traditions. God does not necessarily call us to uniformity even now, but primarily to *the unity of the Spirit.*[2] After all, God is a God of variety. He knows His people and sets them in the Body as it pleases Him. So we should all recognise and respect each other and seek in the Spirit to flow together in oneness, love and grace.

[1] 1 John 1:3. [2] Eph. 4:3.

This is paramount, for Jesus said: *By this shall all men know that ye are my disciples, if ye have love one to another.*[1] Such love recognises no barriers or divisions of the flesh which fragment the people of God. We are joined to Christ the Head, and we are joined to one another in the unity of the Spirit. As in our physical composition, every one of us differs from the other, so in the Body of Christ all members differ from each other, yet it is essential that we recognise the interdependence of each one.

Even within the confines of a single denominational fellowship, some worship God differently from others. We develop our own styles and ways of approaching God and of living in His presence. Uniformity in these things is unnecessary, for the Lord is not terribly interested in our different forms, nor in our outward appearances. God looks on the heart.

Jesus replied to the woman of Samaria who questioned Him about where and how men ought to worship: *The hour cometh, and now is, when the true worshippers shall worship the Father in Spirit and in truth: for the Father seeketh such to worship him. God is a spirit: and they that worship him must worship him in spirit and in truth.*[2] There may never be uniformity, but in the unity of the Spirit everyone will have mutual respect and love.

Church structure

What about organisation and structure? Has God intended a uniform structure for all His people? These questions are not easily answered in the light of the vast variety of administrations and organisations now developed in our different sects and denominations.

It is quite clear to me that elders were appointed to oversee the local Churches established by the early apostles.[3] These were clearly recognised as shepherds of the flock to tend, feed, guard and nurture them.[4] While the spiritual care of the flock was the

[1] John 13:35. [2] John 4:23, 24. [3] Acts 14:23; Titus 1:5. [4] 1 Peter 5:1-4; Acts 20:17, 28-31.

responsibility of the elders, it appears that their domestic, social and material welfare were the concern of the deacons.[1]

The application of shepherding care of the flock may not necessarily be identical in every fellowship. One look at the Antioch new Christian Centre shows how very different it was from the Jerusalem Church in its organisation, and even in how the faith was applied among its people. From the assembly of apostles and elders held at Jerusalem we have a clear indication of that which seemed good both to them and to the Holy Ghost concerning the Churches that were opening up among the Gentile people.[2] It was fully accepted that these would function rather differently from the Church at Jerusalem, at least in matters of conscience.

While God has made all nations of one blood, there are differences of appearance, colour, tradition and culture between most of them. Let us avoid copying each other and be content to be ourselves. We should enjoy the uniqueness of our own cultural differences. So it should be among the people of God. People will differ in their worship from place to place, from culture to culture and from race to race. But there is only one Body of Christ, and in spite of all these superficial differences, we discover that we are bound together in the same bundle of divine life. *Both he that sanctifieth and they who are sanctified are all of one: for which cause he is not ashamed to call them brethren.*[3]

We have to accept this principle of variety in all of God's creation, so why not also in God's redemptive purpose? Then we will be satisfied just to be ourselves, and to accept each other as God made us. Not being uniform in appearance, culture, organisation or structure, will not matter for we know that by

[1] 1 Tim. 3:8; Acts 6:1-4. In this last reference the men were not actually called *Deacons* but they appear to have functioned in that role.

[2] Acts 15. [3] Heb. 2:11.

the Holy Spirit we are all baptised into one Body: *Whether we be Jews or Gentiles, whether we be bond or free; and have been all made to drink into one Spirit.*[1]

Open fellowship

In this way we can share our lives and enjoy the fellowship of the Holy Spirit together. It becomes perfectly possible to relate to one another properly, because the fruit of the Spirit is love, joy, peace, longsuffering, gentleness, goodness, meekness, faith, self-control. We can enjoy and appreciate one another because it is in such fellowship that the fruit of the Spirit is manifested.

In the light of all the things that have historically divided us, denominationally, traditionally and theologically, let us not, at this crucial time in the Church's history, rush to break down or restructure anything unless we are clearly guided by the Lord. It is a very dramatic and even traumatic time of change for some, so we should allow to develop all those things we have been discussing in our consideration of the meaning of submission, such as mutual trust, respect, care and love. We should be faithful and loyal where God has set us, while at the same time allowing the Holy Spirit to give us revelation, and to expand our vision, so that we can identify with one another in the wider Church.

When we break bread we should remember that *we being many are one bread, and one body.*[2] This is how we are meant to consider the fellowship of the Body of Christ at the table of the Lord. In our spirit we identify with our brothers and sisters, and the whole family of God everywhere. We should always remember that we are part of the whole household of faith. This should never mar our commitment and fellowship where we belong in the will of God. Rather, it should become more meaningful, practical and vital in every way, as we mature and grow in grace and in the knowledge of our Lord Jesus Christ, being trans-formed into His likeness and reflecting His glory.

[1] 1 Cor. 12:13. [2] 1 Cor. 10:17.

The emerging Church

In our own local communities all committed believers should seek the face of God till, by the Spirit, we get revelation and vision concerning what the Church in our community should be. We must learn how to relate to each other and how the love that we should have for each other should be shown so that it will be seen by the world that we love one another. If our fellowship is with the Father, with His Son Jesus Christ, and with the Holy Spirit, then we should seek to know what the Spirit of God is doing amongst all believers in our local community.[1] [2]

We have to be practical about the unity of the Body of Christ, and pray and believe for oneness in our particular area. This might call for sacrifice, or even, for some, the laying down of their lives as with the apostle Paul. For others it may require simply the abandonment of unnecessary and irrelevant traditions, and approaching their brothers and sisters so that the local Body begins to function together. For it to come to pass in the wider Church, it must begin in our own locality.

The reigning Church

Only then can we believe for the government of God in our land, and Christ ruling in His Church in the midst of His enemies. This does not imply that the Church is meant to take over national and local government. But what a joy and thrill it will be to see barriers coming down and believers submitting to one another in the fear of God. Then will come a manifestation of the presence of God in the community. The enemy, in all his different forms, will be exposed, and his kingdom in each of our areas unseated; The Lord of glory will be seen to be enthroned, ruling in and through His willing people in this, the day of His power. Then the song, 'Our God Reigns', will take on new meaning.

[1] 1 John 1:3. [2] 2 Cor. 13:14.

Often, what we call the Church in our different communities, is considered by some to be a struggling, weak, ailing institution with no power or authority; worthy only of disregard by the general public. This is certainly not the purpose of God. In the first two or three centuries A.D. Christian believers, with all their simplicity, purity and honesty, posed a major threat to the ruling imperial authorities of Rome and were hounded and martyred for the name of Christ. When there is just and godly government we can approve of it. Otherwise, we must ask: "Does the Church in our city or community present such a threat to our ruling authorities?" It is not necessary for us to become politicians to have ruling authority in our land, any more than the prophet Elijah needed to have political status to bear spiritual authority by which a whole nation was restored and acclaimed that *The Lord, He is the God.*[1]

My vision is of a Church that is not weak and ailing, for Jesus said *I will build My Church.*[2] It is being built now as it advances into the enemy's territory. It is at the gates of hell and they cannot prevail against it. This is the only hope for our nation and for the people of this world. It is God's time to move so that the gospel of the kingdom can be preached in all the world for a witness.

Let us believe now for God to restore vision to His people so that we will be seen to be one in the way that Jesus prayed for us to be one. Only in this way will the fulness of Christ be manifested in the Church which is His Body, the fulness of Him that filleth all in all.[3]

---

[1] 1 Kings 18:39. [2] Matt. 16:18. [3] Eph. 1:23.

18

Submission and Authority in the Local Church

How are we really going to relate together in terms of practical spiritual fellowship? Some believers have problems in submitting to fellow-members in their own group, let alone learning to submit to those of other fellowships. The difficulty for some is crystallised in the statement: "I believe only in submission to God." They seek to listen to God for themselves, then act accordingly in independence and isolation.

If they are truly listening to God He will lead them into fellowship with His people. They will recognise the need for spiritual oversight and of functioning in a co-ordinated way with every other member in the local Church, and thus in the fuller sense in the Body of Christ. Anything else only promotes and perpetuates the confusion, division and fragmentation which has afflicted the Church for centuries. We need to understand the practical implications of submitting to one another in the fear of God in our locality.

Good or bad traditions

We have described the local Church as being the community of people in a particular location who are born again and seeking to walk in the life and fulness of the Holy Spirit. From the moment we endeavour to relate with our brothers and sisters outside our own group, we discover that there are serious problems on account of the variety of denominations and traditions in the one locality.

What of the different creeds and foundation of beliefs to which our various groups subscribe? Much of this, of course, we have inherited from our historical background. It is not my intention to look at this history; although to learn something of it could help us to understand the practical implications of the situations in which we find ourselves.

The pouring out of the Spirit of God in these days is bringing illumination and vision. Holy Spirit enlightenment helps us to see the fleshly nature of all that has served to divide the people of God, and creates a yearning in all our hearts to be rid of such carnality. Vision makes us forward looking, producing within us an inspiration that urges us forward to live in the good of what the Spirit has revealed and to believe for the fulfilment of divine purpose.

The local Church is yet to emerge in the true unity of the Spirit as described in the previous chapter. Let us anticipate this in faith and prepare our hearts willingly to take steps of the Lord's leading towards its fulfilment. In the meantime we should not demand the breakdown of anything that exists, or blunderingly attempt to divide any group, or impose our wills and ideas on existing institutions, man-made or otherwise. Much havoc can be wrought this way and more barriers to fellowship erected as a result. *Except the Lord build the house, they labour in vain that build it.*[1] We need now to walk in the Spirit much more than formerly so that the fruit of love, longsuffering and patience will permeate all our relationships.

Submission and authority are at the heart of a disciplined fellowship, but there can arise very serious problems unless both are exercised in the Holy Spirit. We must be clothed with humility and be subject to one another so that we may learn together in a practical and balanced way. It is vital that we put this into practice in the Church group or fellowship which we belong to at the present time or we will encounter real problems in relating to Christians of other fellowships.

[1] Psalm 127:1.

There is, of course, the possibility that the situations we are in are so entrenched that even after much prayer, heart searching and endeavour to relate in the Spirit, we discover that our spiritual lives are being stifled through lack of true fellowship. Eventually we may have to move out and on. If this is so, we should be thoroughly honest, open and gracious, unafraid to lovingly and humbly testify to God's dealings in our lives. In some instances, this may be the only way in which the true Church of Jesus Christ can emerge.

Spiritual or carnal leadership

There is always great difficulty experienced in this area of submission where carnal minds are involved. When authority becomes autocratic and dominating, and those subject to it are dictated to without due regard to the principles of mutual submission, then serious problems may arise. We have already seen that God is opposed to such an attitude in that He resists the proud but gives grace to the humble.

Paul said: *For though ye have ten thousand instructors in Christ, yet have ye not many fathers: for in Christ Jesus I have begotten you through the gospel. Wherefore I beseech you, be ye followers of me. For this cause have I sent unto you Timotheus, who is my beloved son, and faithful in the Lord, who shall bring you into remembrance of my ways which be in Christ, as I teach every where in every church. Now some are puffed up, as though I would not come to you. But I will come to you shortly, if the Lord will, and will know, not the speech of them which are puffed up, but the power. For the kingdom of God is not in word, but in power. What will ye? shall I come unto you with a rod, or in love, and in the spirit of meekness?* [1]

Here is an example of Paul in his apostleship exercising his spiritual authority in a fatherly way. He said that there may be ten thousand instructors but not many fathers. When we speak

[1] 1 Cor. 4:15-21.

of authority in the local Church, we should not envisage a leader dictating and commanding as though he were a lord over God's heritage. Such authoritarianism never accomplishes anything of an enduring nature.

In a role of responsibility, we are to accept each other in the spirit and grace of our Lord Jesus Christ. Those of us who are leaders and overseers of God's flock are responsible for the immature and younger in the faith, and we should never impose upon them a carnal authority nor exercise a legalistic, dominating discipline over them. Authoritarianism disqualifies a man from responsibility. The only authority that is of God is a spiritual one and reflects the nature of Him who is King of Kings and Lord of Lords.

Carnal authority can be as weak as it can be strong. When it is weak it observes the pitfalls, dangers and faults in others, but will be unable to properly protect, guide, counsel and forewarn them of the dangers that lie ahead. They will be left to go blundering on to disaster. Such leaders are careless and neglectful. Authority that is of the Spirit will so display the nature of Jesus that a rebuke will be given with all gentleness, meekness and love, and people will know that their leaders have their spiritual welfare at heart.

The danger lies in two directions. Overbearing authoritarianism on one hand, or weakness and irresponsibility on the other when we are afraid to correct and admonish. But when we have the father nature, as Paul described, then we will show neither of these extremes. We will have balance in the Spirit of Christ and will graciously bear the authority He has delegated to us. This is not merely the authority of strong words that indicate pride and conceit. Such things will be banished and both authority and power that are of God will be manifest in our speech and instructions.

This applies also to the women who are older and more mature in the faith. Paul is inspired to give direction to both the men and the women when writing to Titus.[1] Women as well as men need guidance, not only about prayer, Bible study and other spiritual activities, but on how to behave normally and practically in the down to earth affairs of every day life. So the more mature women are to teach, train and discipline those who are younger in very practical things: how to behave in marriage, look after a home, keep a family, etc. God does not want us to become 'super-spiritual' so that we cannot apply ourselves to the practicalities of normal living. God created man with the capacity to apply himself in a realistic way to all the demands and issues of life.

By applying ourselves to domestic and workaday tasks in the power of the Spirit there will be grace, purity and beauty displayed in all that we do. We will be aware of the presence of Jesus, and our homes and families will become models to the world around us of the grace, life and blessing of our Lord. The care, instruction, counsel, help and guidance of the young by the spiritually mature can be as important as other kinds of instruction relating to the Word. The disciple of the Lord Jesus is disciplined and this is portrayed in his or her everyday life.

There is a great need for God-ordained leadership at every level in the Church. In recent times, having travelled extensively, it has become most apparent to me that so much of the confusion prevailing among believers is the outcome of a lack of anointed leadership. Paul gave clear guidance to Titus: *In all things showing thyself a pattern of good works; in doctrine showing uncorruptness, gravity, sincerity, sound speech, that cannot be condemned; that he that is of the contrary part may be ashamed, having no evil thing to say of you.*[2]

Concerning his own ministry along with the other itinerant brethren, Paul said: *But (we) have renounced the hidden things of dishonesty, not walking in craftiness, nor handling the word of God deceitfully; but by manifestation of the truth commending ourselves to every man's conscience in the sight of God.*[3]

[1] Titus 2:1-8. [2] Titus 2:7, 8. [3] 2 Cor. 4:2.

Spiritual or carnal reactions

How do believers react when carnal authority is being imposed upon them? Remember that Jesus said that what is of the flesh is flesh. We may expect carnal reactions when there is an imposition of authoritarianism. If we find ourselves under such bondage let us recognise the possibility of this danger and refuse to react in the flesh, condemning and criticising. In the midst of such confusion we should give ourselves to prayer.

If we are aware of long standing imperfections and carnality among those who are over us in our local oversight, we will never change this by carnal reactions nor necessarily by desertion. By the receiving and ongoing infilling of the Holy Spirit we have been endued with the grace of God, and this should enable us to cope in such a situation.

In this chapter I have laid much stress on leadership, for until this operates on a right basis nothing else will. There is also the possibility of carnal attitudes arising among the members of a flock. They may refuse to receive counsel, and may even manifest many of the works of the flesh spoken of by Paul to the *Galatians*.[1] If we are humbly submitted to God and to one another, these things will be exposed and dealt with. Leaders and members alike should ever *walk in the Spirit,*[2] then the promise applies: *Ye shall not fulfil the lust of the flesh.*

The members operating in the dimension of the Holy Spirit will affect those responsible for the ministry and oversight of any Church fellowship. These are the people who will literally portray Christ and through whom vital things can take place. Change must come to God's Church, and for this God has made full provision: *Now unto him that is able to do exceeding abundantly above all that we ask or think, according to the power that worketh in us. Unto him be glory in the church.*[3]

Glory will come because we, whether leading or being led, have the power of the Holy Spirit producing within us such love and grace as will bring change to every willing believer.

[1] Gal. 5:19-21. [2] Gal. 5:16. [3] Eph. 3:20; 21.

Submitting to one another in the fear of God and esteeming others better than ourselves will be more effective than anything else we can do or say.[1]

Faithfulness or compromise

Having said that, it is inevitable that in some cases, tradition: good or bad, scriptural or otherwise, has become so entrenched that any move of the Holy Spirit would be resisted and make the position of spiritual believers quite untenable. Some leaders in certain sections of what calls itself the Church, will adopt an authoritarian and despotic role that Spirit filled believers will find impossible to accept. This was why Stephen suffered martyrdom. His indictment was *Ye do always resist the Holy Ghost.*[2] For the same reason the apostle Paul had occasion to say *I turn from you to the Gentiles. . . .*[3]

The apostle Paul himself was clearly unequivocal and unbending in his stand in such situations. This may pose a problem for believers who are full of the grace of God and who earnestly long to see unity in the Body of Christ. There is no spirit of rebellion in them and they hate to appear insubmissive to those who are over them. For them, this can produce a crisis of conscience.

Are they in danger of compromising their deeply held convictions by becoming subject to carnal directives or expectations? Should an enlightened spiritual believer submit to the 'minister' or church hierarchy in such circumstances? We may go further and ask if it is even possible to submit without themselves having to deny their faith? Would God Himself or His Word direct the believer to submit in such cases?

Once again, taking Paul as an example, he refused to be subject to those who had infiltrated the Church to spy out their liberty.[4] He also refused to submit himself to the apostle Peter's hypocrisy in the case of the Jewish/Gentile controversy in Antioch.[5]

[1] Phil. 2:5. [2] Acts 7:51. [3] Acts 13:46. [4] Gal. 2:4. [5] Gal. 2:11-21.

What is important in such situations is that we are honest, open and full of grace. In the case of Paul and Peter at Antioch there was such honesty and frankness. Refusing to mingle law with grace was paramount to the apostle Paul's ministry. It was obvious, however, that grace prevailed. There was never any real rift in fellowship between Peter and Paul. Years later when Peter was writing an epistle he made reference to his brother apostle thus: *Our beloved brother Paul.*[1]

Honesty and openness in the ministry and in responsible leadership must be clearly evident. There can be no room for any cover-up activity, dishonesty in practice, nor for ulterior motive in the hearts of those who are called to submit one to another in the fear of God.

[1] 2 Peter 3:15.

19

Interdependence

For as we have many members in one body, and all members have not the same office: So we, being many, are one body in Christ, and every one members one of another.[1] For as the body is one, and hath many members, and all the members of that one body, being many, are one body: so also is Christ. For by one Spirit are we all baptised into one body, whether we be Jews or Gentiles, whether we be bond or free; and have been all made to drink into one Spirit. For the body is not one member, but many.[2]

Independent attitude

The spirit of independence in the Body of Christ is totally out of character with the nature of the Lord Jesus. In a physical sense it is inconceivable that any part of one's body should function in total isolation from the others. The human body, being the masterpiece of God's creational glory, fulfils all its complex functions beautifully and in a most balanced and co-ordinated way. God has made us in His image and likeness so that we may reflect the glory of His unity and wholeness.

Distinctive individuality

This does not mean that every member is the same. In fact, the very opposite is the case. Every member of the human body is distinctive and has its own specific function. That is why Paul

[1] Rom. 12:4, 5. [2] 1 Cor. 12:12-14.

said: *Having then gifts differing according to the grace that is given to us.*[1] No two parts of the human body are identical. They are made different from one another for the purpose of complementing each other. God has made us and by His Spirit re-created us just to be ourselves. The lesson is obvious. We should never try to copy one another in our service, nor should we ever be envious or jealous of any other member in the Body of Christ. We each have an individual and distinctive calling and God accepts us as we are by His grace.

Right relationships

Having said that, we clearly cannot function effectively in independence. We are every one members one of another. That is why we have found it necessary to thoroughly examine the meaning of submitting one to another. Fellowship becomes much more meaningful as these principles we have looked at are in evidence. The true spirit of fellowship is seen in the inter-dependence of all its members, and is expressed by unity, openness, respect, trust, care, love, service, discipline, edification and other important graces.

God never intended the members of the Body of Christ to operate in isolation. If we function independently of each other, the rest of the Body suffers. Furthermore, unless there is inter-dependence in the function of all members in the Body, there is an inevitable defectiveness between the members and the Head, who is Christ. A right relationship with Him should inevitably bring us into a right relationship with each other.

The apostle Paul, speaking of this, clearly stated that *Christ is the head of the church: and he is the saviour of the body. . . . Christ also loved the church, and gave himself for it; that he might sanctify and cleanse it with the washing of water by the word. That he might present it to himself a glorious church, not having spot, or wrinkle, or any such thing; but that it should be holy and without blemish.*[2]

[1] Rom. 12:6. [2] Eph. 5:23-27.

Vital interaction

As we look at each other in our respective fellowships we can see many wonderful changes which God has wrought in people's lives. In this process of change it may surprise us if we knew how much effect we have had upon each other. We have helped each other, perhaps far more than we realise.

This should not be a cause for pride for it is only the grace of God that enables us to do anything that is effective and enduring. The only glory that will ever be manifest in God's Church is the glory of His grace. Whether we are receiving or giving in our ministry, function and fellowship: everything is to be to the praise of the glory of His grace alone.

Clearly the concept of the 'Body of Christ' is one in which every member is properly related under the Headship of Christ. This understanding among the spiritually alive committed believers will cause even our times of Breaking of Bread to mean so very much more to us. Paul said: *The bread which we break, is it not the communion of the body of Christ? For we being many are one bread, and one body: for we are all partakers of that one bread.*[1]

Unnecessary deprivation

Eventually we will see more clearly than ever the meaning of this in the wider setting of the Body of Christ. Many small groups and local fellowships are impoverished because they stand in need of vital ministries of the ascended Christ and gifts of the Holy Ghost. While these gifts are functioning in the Body, some are deprived of them because of a spirit of independence, isolationism and sometimes mistrust.

It is sad that some have been so preoccupied with building their own kingdoms, empires, ecclesiastical structures and movements that they continue to remain isolated. This is a cause of much deprivation in many fellowships. I reiterate that many

[1] 1 Cor. 10:16, 17.

of these essential ministries are currently in existence, but they are either unavailable because of imposed man-made limitations or they are unwelcome because of an unhealthy spirit of independence among those who have the need.

The idea that any 'minister' of a congregation can fulfil all the roles outlined in the Ephesian and Roman epistles, is utterly foreign to the teaching of the Word of God and not in harmony with divine purpose for the Church at any time.[1]

Divine intention

It is the divine intention that *we all come in the unity of the faith, and of the knowledge of the Son of God, unto a perfect man, unto the measure of the stature of the fulness of Christ.*[2] This will surely be accomplished. The barriers hindering true fellowship and restricting the full flow and availability of all the vital Christ gifted ministries will yet be swept away by the opening of the floodgates of real Holy Ghost blessing upon the Church.

When Jesus prayed that prayer for unity it was for the express purpose: *that the world might believe that thou hast sent me.*[3] The Church has not yet had the impact on the world that it should have because of divisiveness and fragmentation. Jesus longed for the whole Church to be seen to be one. Only in this way can there be a revelation of Christ in all His fulness, in terms that this world can understand.

Jesus prayed *That the world might believe.* Let us not shrug our shoulders in disbelief at such an apparent impossibility. Jesus did not pray futile prayers nor did He ever waste a word. He gave Himself for a Church that would be without spot or wrinkle or any such thing. **A Glorious Church.**

[1] Eph. 4:11; Rom. 12:6-8. [2] Eph. 4:13. [3] John 17:21.

20

Divine Order

Everything God does is in accordance with divine order. He is not haphazard, disorderly or careless. Since He has an eternal purpose for the Church, we can be sure that there is a discipline and order about it that is unique and incomparable. At the moment the Church does not always reflect this, especially when so many of us are doing what seems to be right in our own eyes.

Because He is a God of order, says Paul, *God set the members every one of them in the body, as it hath pleased him.*[1] That word 'set' means that He has placed them there, every member, by order, design and purpose. In this way God has provided the necessary responsible ministries: *And God hath set some in the church, first apostles, secondarily prophets, thirdly teachers, after that miracles, then gifts of healings, helps, governments, diversities of tongues.*[2]

The need for order

Tragically, many of us have not seen the need for God's order. We have been inclined to set up our own institutions and have become dislocated. While believers have been careless about God's order, the enemy of Christ and His Church has systematically proceeded with his own plans, with calculated deception and cunning in all his practices. We have to confess that disorder in the Church has provided much ground for exploitation by the enemy.

[1] 1 Cor. 12:18. [2] 1 Cor. 12:28.

Yet we can take heart, for this is not how the Church is going to remain. Jesus said *I will build my church,*[1] and He is doing just that. He is putting its members together and will yet bring order out of chaos. Reference has been made to the vision of David in the Psalms. God's willing people are portrayed as an army virile with youth, standing shoulder to shoulder in holy array, through which Christ the Lord rules now in the midst of His enemies.[2] For this purpose He has equipped His servants with spiritual authority. They are rising in the power of the Holy Spirit to lead God's army forward from strength to strength, from victory to victory, so that this gospel of the kingdom, of kingdom life, authority and power can be preached in all the world for a witness before the end comes.[3]

By grace alone

What a miracle of the grace of God is this! Human beings, marred by sin, deceived by the powers of darkness, unfit and unholy, without God and without hope, in bondage to sin and evil powers—now transformed, released and saved! All their sin, weakness, corruption and bondage Jesus took on Himself at the cross. After descending into Hades He rose again from the dead and ascended up on high, having the keys of hell and of death and taking captive with Him a captive multitude. Such was the nature of the finished work of Christ that fallen, sinful men have been willingly and joyously captivated by Him, completely releasing them from bondage under Satan's domination. By the regeneration of the Spirit they themselves have become gifts of the ascended Christ to the Church, reflecting the grace and glory of His Headship.

Apostles, prophets, evangelists, pastors and teachers are specific gifts with clearly defined ministries, but every member of the Body has been described as a gift of Christ to His Church.

[1] Matt. 15:18. [2] Psalm 110:3. [3] Matt. 24:14.

But to every one has been given grace according to the measure of the gift of Christ.[1] It is quite clear that some are specifically called and equipped for the responsibilities of leadership, headship, government and rule in the Body of Christ. All by the grace of God alone.

Responsible oversight

Amongst other things, God has set governments in the Church. For this reason the apostle Peter instructs the elders of the flock of God to take the oversight.[2] In the epistle to the Hebrews we are exhorted: *Obey them that have the rule over you, and submit yourselves: for they watch for your souls, as they that must give account, that they may do it with joy, and not with grief: for that is unprofitable for you.*[3]

Responsible ministries are given to the Body for the perfecting of the saints so that they can all fulfil their work of service, to the mutual upbuilding of the whole Body. If they are already called saints, i.e. holy ones, why do they need such ministries to perfect and mature them? It is because this is how God sees the believer in Christ. In Him He sees His people as perfect, but the outworking of that indicates what great need there is in all lives to come into the realisation of all that God has called us to and for which He has made full provision.

Bondservants of Christ

Let us look a little more closely at this text: *When He ascended up on high He led captivity captive (or He led captive a captive multitude).*[4] The statement here is a quotation from one of David's Messianic Psalms and in the Authorised Version is expressed as follows: *Thou hast ascended on high, thou hast led captivity captive: thou hast received gifts for men; yea, for the rebellious also, that the Lord God might dwell among them.*[5]

[1] Eph. 4:7. [2] 1 Peter 5:2. [3] Heb. 13:17. [4] Eph. 4:8. [5] Psalm 68:18.

Clearly, the rebellious ones have been captivated by the ascended Christ, and have themselves become the recipients of His marvellous grace. This is how Paul saw himself and referred continuously to his being *a prisoner of Jesus Christ,* His bond-slave. He was captivated by Him. He was one of that captive multitude whom Jesus led forth in His triumphant ascension.

Ye are not your own, for ye are bought with a price.[1] This means that in redemption He bought us with His own blood out of captivity to Satan and sin's bondage; out of the condemnation of God's holy law and its just demands and penalty; and that He purchased us to be His own bondslaves, for He desired to have us for Himself.

What a glorious captivity: captivated by love, grace, truth, honour and the dignity of true manhood again; restored to dominion under His pre-eminent rule and authority to be our true selves; to be conformed to His image, share in His eternal programme and to be part of His glorious Church, the revelation of the fulness of Him *that filleth all in all.*

David in that Psalm prophetically unfolds the divine purpose: *That the Lord might dwell among them.* Paul said that He *ascended up far above all heavens, that He might fill all things.*[2] Mankind will yet know that God dwells victoriously in reigning power among His people.

All are involved

This captive multitude He has gifted to be members in the Body. Some He has given as men of apostolic authority; some with prophetic insight; others with evangelistic fervour; some with pastoral and shepherding care; and others with a teaching ability to instruct the saints of God. Through these gifts of Christ, all the saints will be perfected to fulfil their work of ministry in co-ordination with the rest of the Body.

[1] 1 Cor. 5:19, 20. [2] Eph. 4:10.

There is a very real sense in which every member of the Body is in the ministry, called to be a minister of the sanctuary; called to offer sacrifices and praises to Him who has called us out of darkness into His most marvellous light. Since He has made us kings and priests unto our God we can all sing those beautiful words:

> Come and praise Him royal priesthood,
> Come and worship holy nation.

So God has established order in the Body and given specific gifts to the Body to the end that every member will be perfected to become a functioning part of the Body. Nobody is called only to occupy a pew once or twice a week. All are given grace to function in their respective callings.

It is very important to understand this, since it creates a more equitable distribution of responsibility within the Church, and those given the role of leadership and rule are relieved of unnecessary burden. This should bring home to everyone a personal sense of commitment to God and to each other. In God's order every member of the Body is called to act responsibly. Whatever our calling in the fellowship, it is vital that we pray for, counsel and support each other. No one should experience any difficulty in being able to function in the capacity to which he has been called, for grace has been given to each one according to the measure of the gift. Conversely, no one should ever be burdened with responsibilities for which he has not received grace.

There is always an imbalance when certain parts of our body are not functioning. So it is in the Body of Christ. It was never the purpose of God that there should be a 'clergy' having all the responsibility and a 'laity' who are mere spectators and listeners.

Headship demonstrated

It has already been pointed out that apostles, prophets, evangelists, pastors and teachers are given to perfect the saints.

These gifts of the ascended Christ are called and anointed by the Holy Spirit for their service. The New Testament gives proof of this.[1] God Himself has ordained that the Headship of Christ is to be manifested in the Church, and it is through these gifts He has ordained that it should be demonstrated.

Our Lord Jesus Christ has the authority and power to do this because in His triumphal ascension He established Himself as Head over all principality, power, might and dominion on our behalf. All authority in heaven and on earth is His and He has vested that Headship in the Church which is His Body, the fulness of Him who filleth all in all.[2] All gifts of authority in the Body can only operate as they reflect Him in His Headship; bearing the marks and revealing the nature of His authority. We are reminded of the way in which he took the towel and washed the disciples' feet, and said that if He, our Lord and Master can do this, so ought we to do one to another.[3] The nature of God's order in His Church is very different from normal human organisation.

Reflecting Christ

The headship of Christ is reflected, not only in these specific ministries, but through the whole Body. The whole of God's Church is called to portray spiritual authority. We should give thanks to God for those whom He has called to reflect His Headship in the Body.

We should remember, however, that no apostle will ever be recognised as such unless he reflects Him who is the chief apostle. The same can be said of prophets, evangelists, pastors and teachers. Whatever our calling, or whatever the label by which we may be known, it can only be valid according to the degree to which we reflect that particular aspect of the character and ministry of Christ Himself. He is the summation of all the gifts and callings. The only headship in the Body that has any authority and power is that which reflects the Headship of Christ.

[1] Acts 13:1-3; Rom. 12:6; 2 Cor. 3:5, 6. [2] Eph. 1:23. [3] John 13:14.

This applies similarly to the elders who are called to take the oversight of the flock. They are to be responsible for it, exercising the authority of His shepherding care. Jesus talked to Peter about this very thing after His resurrection. He said 'if you love Me, Peter, shepherd My sheep, feed and care for My lambs.' This means that such men have to nurture, feed, guide, lead and shepherd them under Him who is the Chief Shepherd.

With reference to such leaders, those who are being led are exhorted to: *Obey them that have the rule over you, and submit yourselves.* **For they watch for your souls as they that must give account,** *that they may do it with joy, and not with grief; for that is unprofitable for you.*[1]

Since it is God Himself who has established oversight in His Church under the Headship of Christ, and since that oversight has only spiritual authority in which to function, spiritually minded people will recognise and submit to it. Others will rebel, resist, go their own way, do as they like and lead other immature and young believers astray. Failure to submit to God ordained oversight makes it impossible for that oversight to function properly in whatever area the rebellion exists.

This is not a man-appointed oversight, nor does it bear carnal authority. This is God ordained oversight as Paul reminded the Ephesian elders: *Take heed, therefore, unto yourselves, and to all the flock, over which* **the Holy Ghost hath made you overseers,** *to feed the Church of God, which He hath purchased with His own blood.*[2]

[1] Heb. 13:17. [2] Acts 20:28.

21

The Authority of Apostleship

Submitting to an apostle

To which apostle do **you** submit? A loaded question; but I am not so sure that it is either valid or even scriptural. However, it is a question that is being asked of many these days.

Do you recognise apostles today? This is a valid question, and scriptural too. In this case the relevant question should be "Do you submit to apostleship?"

There is a vast difference between the first question and the last. It is possible for a man to call himself an apostle, or even for a body of people to set him up as one, yet he himself have no apostolic calling. He may be a leader, superintendent, administrator or even a pastor, but if he is not an apostle we should not call him such. To the Church at Ephesus, the risen, ascended Lord said, *And thou hast tried them which say they are apostles, and are not, and hast found them liars.*[1] For this, at least, He commended them.

If the first question were a valid one: "To which apostle do **you** submit?" the inherent dangers for any apostle so nominated would be obvious to all. There are personal pitfalls like pride and exclusivism, as well as more general temptations such as subjugating those in submission creating party spirit and division, and even possibly depriving others of their own ministry and function.

Apostles and elders

It seems very clear from the New Testament that government in the local Church is by God-appointed elders. There are several

[1] Rev. 2:2.

references to this.[1] Paul also spoke of it in the plural: *Governments*.[2] In each locality we should expect local spiritual government and oversight for the flock of God.

The ascended Christ also gifted apostles, prophets, etc. to the Church who clearly have an important role in the government of the wider Church. They have the authority and responsibility to appoint and ordain elders; teach and guide them; exhort and counsel them; cover and co-operate with them. The elders of the New Testament Churches were the product of anointed apostolic ministry who in turn recognised and respected their apostleship.

It is interesting to note that the only council assembly referred to in the New Testament Church was composed of apostles and elders.[3] Its remit was to resolve the problem of the application of Judaistic tradition relating to the law of Moses and circumcision by Gentile converts and Churches.[4]

The council was concerned only with the spiritual welfare of the people. Its objective was to give directives mutually agreed between the apostles and elders which were in harmony with the guidance of the Holy Spirit. Thus they could say *It seemed good to the Holy Ghost and to us. . . .*[5] The whole Church also were in full agreement with the final decisions.

Whose servants?

We should always remember that government in the Church of Jesus Christ is very different from that of secular organisations. Paul called himself *a servant (bondslave) of Jesus Christ*.[6] To the saints at Corinth he said *For we preach not ourselves, but Christ Jesus the Lord; and ourselves your servants for Jesus' sake.*[7]

The major difference is that, whereas in a secular society academic qualifications are of primary importance, in the Church the first essential qualification is spiritual, for one's

[1] Acts 14:23; 20:28. 1 Tim. 3:1-7; 1 Tim. 5:1, 2; Titus 1:5-9; 2:1-5; 1 Thess. 5:12, 13; Heb. 13:7, 17, 24; James 5:14; 1 Peter 5:1-5.

[2] 1 Cor. 12:28. [3] Acts 15:2, 6. [4] Acts 15:1, 5. [5] Acts 15:28. [6] Eph. 3:1; 4:1. [7] 2 Cor. 4:5.

calling must be wholly of God. Only by the Holy Spirit can we effectively and fruitfully function in the Church. In other organisations it is essential that there be an appointment of offices in a hierarchical order or chain of command. In the Church, structures of this kind are man-made. Jesus said *If any man desire to be first, the same shall be last of all, and servant of all.*[1]

Authority in the anointing

Leaders in the Church are only leaders because the ascended Christ gifted them and bestowed grace upon them proportionate to the measure of the gift. They bear leadership and government responsibility, but only in the Spirit. The moment they cease to function in the Holy Spirit, they lose their authority.

The reason for much confusion in the Church is that men have set themselves up, or have been set up by others, as governing authorities. Authoritarianism and its resultant carnal directives cause confusion, frustration and fragmentation in the Body.

Government in the local Church is by elders. Government in the wider setting of the Body of Christ should include apostles and prophets who will be able to minister wisdom and revelation to the elders. But in neither case is there the slightest suggestion in the Scriptures that such government is institutional, hierarchical or purely administrative. It is the Holy Spirit who calls and sets elders to oversee the flock of God.[2] Likewise when Paul and Barnabas were sent forth to fulfil their apostolic calling they were sent forth by the Holy Ghost, with the full recognition and co-operation of the other brethren.[3]

Even a brief examination of the ministries of these men reveals that the authority they possessed and exercised was only that of the Spirit. Any other kind of authority would have been exposed for what it was when confronting demonic situations.

[1] Mark 9:35. [2] Acts 20. [3] Acts 13.

If it had been carnal authority they would have needed to impose it in a dominating, dictatorial and legalistic manner. But these men had such spiritual authority that people stood in awe, and were moved by a sense of the fear of God.

Apostle of Jesus Christ

Apostolic authority is valid only when exercised in the context of the true meaning of apostleship. Paul referred to himself as *An apostle of Jesus Christ,*[1] and to the Galatians was most specific: *Not of men, neither by man, but by Jesus Christ, and God the Father, who raised him from the dead.*

The meaning of the word 'apostle' is 'one sent'. He is a special messenger sent of Jesus Christ. He can function in his apostleship only as he operates within the terms of his calling and commission, i.e. the wisdom, grace, will and authority of the sender, the Lord Jesus Christ. Jesus said *The servant is not greater than his lord.*[2]

To blindly submit to a man who bears the label 'apostle' is unscriptural and dangerous. Being compelled to submit by whatever influence, or even feeling constrained to, may imply that the apostle's authority is considered to be infallible. Conversely, submission to him may be thought justifiable on the grounds that, whether he is right or wrong, the responsibility for the consequences lies with him.

The errors of this approach are obvious. Regardless of his spiritual status no man is infallible. I do not say that cynically, but in love, to warn my brothers and sisters of the danger. It also places more authority and responsibility on him than is good for him. There is also the danger of depriving those who thus submit to him of the right to think and decide for themselves, even in personal matters.

[1] 1 Cor. 1:1; 2 Cor. 1:1; Gal. 1:1. et. al. [2] Matt. 10:24.

There is no problem with an apostle who functions in the nature of true apostleship. His responsibility is to live constantly in the anointing that sets him apart to his calling. His apostleship is of Jesus Christ, by the will of God, and in the Holy Ghost. If he functions 'out of the spirit' and 'in the flesh' his spiritual authority is nil and he is as susceptible to error and heresy as any other person. At no time are the members of the Body of Christ called upon to submit to such. All members of the Body who are truly walking in the Spirit will recognise the spiritual authority of the apostle who functions in the anointing, and will gladly submit to that authority which is truly of the Lord.

22

Headship

Headship in marriage

But I would have you to know, that the head of every man is Christ; and the head of the woman is the man; and the head of Christ is God.[1]

It is of vital importance that we seek to understand headship as taught in the Word of God. If we harbour doubts about its relevance and conclude that the subject is archaic or medieval and not now applicable in this modern age and generation, then we shall become unbalanced, miss the purpose of God and lose the blessing of His authority and the covering of His Headship in the Church, now so desperately needed. A most beautiful example of this is portrayed in Christian marriage.

Wives are exhorted to: *Submit yourselves unto your own husbands, as unto the Lord.*[2] Some people have expressed antagonism to Paul for this, implying that he was some sort of male chauvinist. He was not alone, however, in this kind of instruction. Peter also exhorts: *Likewise, ye wives, be in subjection to your husbands; . . . For after this manner in the old time the holy women also, who trusted in God, adorned themselves, being in subjection unto their own husbands.*[3]

It is recorded that after man's fall in the garden of Eden: *Unto the woman he said, . . . thy desire shall be to thy husband, and he shall rule over thee.*[4] Why did God make this pronouncement on the woman? Some have imagined that God showed respect of persons, making the woman inferior to the man. But is it really a question of inequality, or partiality? Not at all!

[1] 1 Cor. 11:3. [2] Eph. 5:22. [3] 1 Peter 3:1, 5. [4] Gen. 3:16.

The covering of headship

God is a God of order. In all societies there must be authority that can govern, maintain order, bear responsibility and interpret what is lawful. Government is necessary also for defence, security and protection. Leadership for guidance and control in all the affairs relating to society is essential. Similarly, both in marriage and in the Church, God has established Headship.

True appreciation of both the nature and function of Headship is exceedingly important. Failure to understand, or having a distorted understanding will cause some to evade its issues, and others to react in rebellion. The twentieth century is characterised by rebellion against any form of authority, and our society is heading quickly towards anarchy. In the Church, this spirit brings chaos, and in marriage, dissolution.

The custom and symbolism of head covering taught by Paul in the Corinthian epistle is all to do with Headship.[1] The Headship or covering of Christ the Messiah, was God the Father. Hence you see Him in constant communion with His Father, having come, not to do His own will, but the will of Him that sent Him. *I do nothing of myself, but as my Father hath taught me. . . .*[2] Jesus was in total submission to His Father's will.

The Headship of Christ

The head of every man is Christ. The man who is not submitted to Christ as his Lord and under His Headship, is without a God-ordained covering. Such a man is exposed to the intrigue and whims of others or to the subtle deceptions of Satan and his hosts.

James says that if we **submit** to God, then we can **resist** the devil and he will flee from us.[3] Being subject to Christ means that we have the covering of One who is Lord of all. He has dealt with every area of mankind's complex problems. He grappled with all the unholy operations of satanic principalities and powers at Calvary and routed them. All authorities are now

[1] 1 Cor. 11:1-16. [2] John 8:28. [3] James 4:7.

under His feet. He reigns supreme and is Lord of all. All power and all authority in heaven and in earth are in His hands. To become subject to Him means we have the covering of the One in whose hands is universal authority.

The role of women

What about women then? Cannot a woman submit herself to Christ directly without having to subject herself to any man? Is it not true that *There is neither Jew nor Greek, there is neither bond nor free, there is neither male nor female: for ye are all one in Christ Jesus?* [1]

It is very evident from all the Scriptures that women have as important a place in God's care and love as men. There is not the slightest hint of women being inferior, second-class or incapable of controlling their own affairs under Christ. Throughout the Bible, women are given ample place and scope. It is upon both men and women that the Spirit of God is being poured according to the promise of Joel and confirmed by Peter. [2] [3] Both men and women are given the gifts of the Spirit and are called of God to function in prayer and prophecy in the Church. The Word of God does not teach that any man, other than the Man Christ Jesus, is the mediator between women and God.

Women laboured with the apostle Paul in the gospel. [4] Philip the evangelist had four daughters who prophesied. [5] Priscilla, as well as Aquila, taught and expounded unto Apollos, the apostle, the way of God more perfectly. [6] Both Aquila and Priscilla are quoted by the apostle Paul as being his helpers in Christ Jesus. [7] Phoebe is referred to as a deaconess of the Church and the saints are asked to assist her in all her business and service. [8]

It is important that we understand the nature and function of Headship. God has not ordained woman for the role of headship. That role He has given to man. God has ordained woman

[1] Gal. 3:28. [2] Joel 2:28, 29. [3] Acts 2:17, 18. [4] Phil. 4:3. [5] Acts 21:8, 9. [6] Acts 18:24-26. [7] Rom. 16:3. [8] Rom. 16:1, 2.

for other functions, but not that of headship. And just as Christ was submitted to the Headship of His Father, and man is submitted to the Headship of Christ, so the head of the woman is the man.[1] Just as there is no inequality between Father, Son and Spirit in the Godhead—so it is in the relationship of husband and wife.

Paul deals with the nature of that headship in the marriage situation. *Wives, submit yourselves unto your own husbands as unto the Lord. For the husband is the head of the wife, even as Christ is the head of the church. . . . Husbands, love your wives, even as Christ also loved the church, and gave himself for it.*[2] Here we are given a clear insight into the nature of the Headship of Christ. It is definitely not one of authoritarianism, dictatorialism, domination or autocracy. It is a Headship immersed in love—total, selfless, sacrificial, divine love.

The apostle Paul finally brings us right back to God's original intention for marriage: *For this cause shall a man leave his father and mother, and shall be joined unto his wife, and they two shall be one flesh. This is a great mystery: but I speak concerning Christ and the church.*[3] Both the submission of the wife and the headship of the husband, functioning only in pure love, make for the perfect unity that God intended in marriage.

This is a mystery, said Paul. Yes, but it is the most beautiful illustration of the relationship existing between the Body of Christ and its Head. When every Christian marriage is bound together in this way, then the Church will begin to manifest the glory He purposed and for which Christ gave Himself.

The Church is subject to Christ because He loved it. He is its Saviour and protector; its defence; its safety and security; its governing authority; its victory; its life and power. What a beautiful and perfect design for His Church! He shall present it to Himself a glorious Church; spotless, pure and resplendent, and the Church's response of love will be in wholehearted submission to Him.

[1] 1 Cor. 11:3. [2] Eph. 5:22-25. [3] Eph. 5:31, 32.

This is how Christian marriage should be. The believing husband has the nature and life of Jesus in him. He accepts his role and responsibility of headship. This headship is immersed in love; gracious, caring, protecting, sacrificing, covering love. His aim will be to present his bride to himself and before all as someone of glory, beauty and purity; wholesome in every way and more glorious than she could ever be without him.

Of course, submission in marriage is not totally one way. Each submits to the other in sharing their problems, in discussing marital affairs, desires and purposes, and even in assisting each other in arriving at decisions. There is total openness, trust, care, understanding and discipline. All the things we have described in the principles of submission one to another apply to the marriage bond but in his God-given role of headship the man is held accountable to God. It is he who bears responsibility for the affairs of his marriage and family. God has ordained it thus.

Headship for the unmarried

What about the unmarried women? Who assumes the responsibility of headship and the covering this is designed to provide for them? Surely that is what the Church is for. The unmarried women are covered by headship in the Body of Christ, as are all members of that Body. We all need headship. We all need covering.

In this teaching from the Word of God on submission in marriage there is a qualifying phrase: *Wives, submit yourselves unto your own husbands, as unto the Lord.* This clearly handles the problem of the husband becoming a dictator, tyrant, or oppressor. No woman is commanded to subject herself to that. Her submission is in the fear of God; in the Spirit of Christ; as unto the Lord. Submission on her part presupposes the headship of love on him.

Headship in the Church

We can be sure that Headship in the Body will not become autocratic, authoritarian and dominating, for all will be clothed with humility and be subject one to another. For it is the Headship of Christ that is in the Church. His Headship is not only **over the Church** but **over all things to the Church.** Just as a human body expresses what is in its head so does the Body of Christ. The natural co-ordinated relationship displayed in the human body is analogous to submission in the Church.

Government in the Church is the authority of Him who is Head delegated to men ordained by Him. There is no way in which men can exercise authority of Headship that is out of character with the nature of Christ who has delegated it. If they do, they are false. These men should not be feared.

Any servant of God who is truly a gift of the ascended Christ to the Church, whether apostle, prophet, evangelist, pastor or teacher, if he is walking humbly with God, and anointed by the Holy Spirit, will bear the hallmark of divine authority.[1]

Submission of apostles

Humility will identify him as he submits his revelation to others who are in authority and oversight in the location to which God sends him. His words will be recognised as the wisdom of the Lord by those who are given responsibility, if they too are functioning in the realm of God's grace and are themselves proved to be humble men of God. If he is rejected by carnal eldership, then God will deal with those men to whom he has submitted his revelation, or remove the candlestick (church) from that place.

Any servant of God clothed with humility, will not be afraid to have his revelation or instruction examined or proved by other mature men. We may well ask, of course, about Paul who,

[1] Eph. 4:11.

rather than submit to Peter in his dissimulation, *withstood him to the face.*[1] When we examine the case we see that there was no question of disagreement over doctrine, nor was there even a desire in the heart of Paul to dictate to Peter in some authoritative or dominating way. Paul was in conflict here with a glaring example of hypocrisy on Peter's part. His behaviour adversely affected his other brethren, and indeed the whole Church, bringing them into bondage. Paul could not overlook it. There is ample evidence that, normally, in matters of conscience, conduct and discipline in the Church, the apostles and elders submitted to one another.

[1] Gal. 2:11-17.

23

Members' Function

For as we have many members in one body, and all members have not the same office; so we, being many, are one body in Christ, and every one members one of another.[1]

Variety of function

That word 'office' translates a word that really means 'function'. *All members have not the same function.* So for any member to be able to function correctly it is essential that he is in his rightful place, properly joined to and co-ordinated with the rest of the Body. The teaching of Paul is that not one member can say to another *I have no need of you. Nay, much more those members of the body, which seem to be more feeble, are necessary . . . that there should be no schism in the body.*[2]

In the Ephesian epistle we are reminded that when all the members are together, growing up into Christ the Head, and fitly joined together, compacted by that which every joint supplies, *According to the effectual working in the measure of every part,*[3] then there is increase and building up of the body in love.

Basis for function

As each member is happily prepared to submit to others and to headship in the Body, only then is there freedom for them to function in the way that God has purposed. Apostles, pastors or elders should never exercise carnal authority in the Body. In the spirit of humility and grace, all leaders and members alike should

[1] Rom. 12:4, 5. [2] 1 Cor. 12:21-25. [3] Eph. 4:16.

work in perfect harmony together. The headship vested in these ministry gifts is not for the purpose of lording it over the Body, but rather for the perfecting of the saints *for them to fulfil their work of ministry.* Every member is called to a particular function.

Most of the epistles were written, not to the elders of the Churches, but to all the flock of God. All were to know their place and function in the Body. All should be encouraged to grow in grace and in the knowledge of our Lord Jesus Christ. Paul prayed for all the saints and faithful at Ephesus that they might receive the Spirit of wisdom and revelation in the knowledge of God—and that the eyes of their understanding might be enlightened.[1]

Preparation for function

The charge made concerning all the saints as recorded in the epistle to the Hebrews is: *When for the time ye ought to be teachers, ye have need that one teach you again which be the first principles of the oracles of God.*[2] This was really an indictment that the saints were not growing in the knowledge of God and were insensitive to His voice. All believers should be encouraged to develop a vitally intimate relationship with the Lord. Only then will they be able to function as they should in the fellowship.

It has been said that the minister, or shepherd, or apostle (or whoever is in authority) is responsible for hearing God's voice for the sheep. It may be that the very young and immature will take some time to develop sensitivity in this area. Some unwise and confused people may need assurance and help in matters of divine guidance through their leaders—but this is never intended to be the norm. The Lord delights in two-way communion with all His people.

[1] Eph. 1:17-19. [2] Heb. 5:12.

Guidance in function

To the shepherds of God's flock, at Ephesus, Paul instructs as follows: *Take heed therefore unto yourselves, and to all the flock, over the which the Holy Ghost hath made you overseers, to feed the church of God, which he purchased with his own blood.*[1] He then spoke of the possibility of grievous wolves entering in and not sparing the flock and men arising from among themselves, speaking perversely and seeking to draw away disciples after them.

God has appointed shepherds that they may take care of the flock by protection, guidance and leadership. They are responsible for the spiritual development of the flock since their stewardship is ordained of God.

As with the apostles, so with the elders: their authority must be that which comes from the anointing of the Holy Spirit. Otherwise they will have an adverse effect on people who are seeking to function and flow in the life of the Spirit. There is a great need for release among the people of God in the gifts of the Spirit (charismata). Diligent oversight is required to encourage the members to pray and believe for this. All the gifts spoken of in the Corinthian epistle are available and should be operating in the Church. *All these (gifts) worketh that one and the selfsame Spirit, dividing to every man severally (separately) as he will.*[2]

Release in function

Any suggestion of unnecessary limitations that may crush signs of emerging spiritual life in the flock or hinder growth and legitimate function should never be entertained either by leaders or those who are being led.

Instruction regarding control in the use of spiritual gifts in the assembly, as outlined by Paul to the Corinthians, were certainly never intended to bring bondage to the Church.[3] These were given as a guide to safeguard the fellowship from the abuse of

[1] Acts 20:28. [2] 1 Cor. 12:11. [3] 1 Cor. 14.

gifts, and to avoid unhealthy spiritual exercises and uncontrolled excesses that are purposeless. Paul's earnest appeal is that all the members should seek to excel to the edifying of the Church.

God's people everywhere need the encouragement of the operation of these gifts in the Church. No one should feel stifled. If mutual submission is practised correctly in the Body, then due respect will be displayed by both the oversight and the members. But when there is a carnal display and questionable use of spiritual gifts as well as either a dominating or weak and undiscerning oversight, members in the fellowship become uneasy and feel insecure. Confusion will ensue as a result and we should always remember that *God is not the author of confusion, but of peace.*[1]

Maturing in function

Since it is God Himself who established oversight in the Church, under the Headship of Christ, and since that oversight has only a spiritual authority in which to function, spiritually-minded people will submit to it. In this atmosphere we should not be in bondage because of our immaturity. Maturity comes with practice. We should not be afraid to make mistakes provided we are humbly willing to be corrected when we do.[2]

[1] 1 Cor. 14:33. [2] Heb. 5:12-14.

24

Authority in Conflict

One of the most grievous results of disunity in the Church through insubmissiveness is that the members of the Body become vulnerable to attack from the powers of darkness. This is much more prevalent than most of us realise.

Peter exhorts: *Be sober, be vigilant; because your adversary the devil, as a roaring lion, walketh about, seeking whom he may devour.*[1] Paul exhorts: *Put on the whole armour of God, that ye may be able to stand against the wiles of the devil. For we wrestle not against flesh and blood, but against principalities, against powers, against the rulers of the darkness of this world, against spiritual wickedness in high places.*[2]

What is very significant in both these Scriptures which deal with spiritual conflict, is that the context concerns mutual submission. When we are not thus submitted we are out of our God-ordained setting and in some way dislocated from fellowship. It is then that we become prey for our adversary.

Under the covering of Headship in the Body we are protected and secure. This is essentially because Christ Himself is the Head over all things **to the Church.** Since that Headship is *to the Church,* this means He has vested its authority in the Church. We cannot know the full authority of Christ our Head if we are dislocated from true fellowship in the Body. Even when we are alone, as missionaries, for instance, often are, if we know our setting in the Body and submit, relate and function there, then we are not disfellowshipped from the vital unity of the Spirit.

[1] 1 Peter 5:8. [2] Eph. 6:11, 12.

It is on the basis of our submitting one to another in the fear of God that we are exhorted to resist our adversary steadfast in the faith. On the same basis we are exhorted: *Be strong in the Lord and in the power of his might. Put on the whole armour of God.*

In the Psalms we have a beautiful prophetic insight into the day of God's power when Christ's Church is seen to be standing together as an army in holy array, expressing the authority of the risen, ascended Lord and manifesting a royal priestly ministry in the Name of Him who hath an eternally unchanging priesthood.[1] Both the Lordship and Priesthood of Christ are reflected in God's willing people. They are seen as His united Church joined to Christ its Head. Through the Church He rules and reigns in the midst of His enemies. What a picture of His totally victorious, overcoming Church.

Not one individual in that triumphant army of the Lord is pressed into His service. Everyone is willing in the day of God's power. It is this yieldedness, willingness and obedience of faith that makes the Church what God has called it to be.

If there are problems regarding submission they are in this area of willingness more than any other. Once we have the victory in this we will not only **see** the Church glorious and triumphant in the face of every evil onslaught, but we will **share** in the thrill of it. No more weakness, fear or failure. We will participate in the life, power and glory of our risen, ascended Lord who is Head over all things to the Church which is His Body, the fulness of Him who filleth all in all.

---

[1] Psalm 110.